# Karma Dharma and Meditation

by

Devi Dayal Agarwal

**Gotham Books**

30 N Gould St.
Ste. 20820, Sheridan, WY 82801
https://gothambooksinc.com/

Phone: 1 (307) 464-7800

© 2023 *Devi Dayal Agarwal*. All rights reserved.

No part of this book may be reproduced, stored in a retrieval system, or transmitted by any means without the written permission of the author.

Published by Gotham Books (June 1, 2023)

ISBN: 979-8-88775-312-6 (P)
ISBN: 979-8-88775-313-3 (E)

Because of the dynamic nature of the Internet, any web addresses or links contained in this book may have changed since publication and may no longer be valid.

The views expressed in this work are solely those of the author and do not necessarily reflect the views of the publisher, and the publisher hereby disclaims any responsibility for them.

# CONTENTS

Preface .................................................................................................. 1
List of Hindi Words with English Translation ................................... 3

## SECTION I: KARMA and DHARMA

Chapter I: Introduction ........................................................................ 1
Chapter II: Ethicisation of Actions ..................................................... 8
Chapter III: Relationship Between Actions, Death & Birth ............ 16
Chapter IV: Varanashrama System ................................................... 23
Chapter V: Arjuna's Misgivings ......................................................... 35
Chapter VI: Krishna's Advice ............................................................. 41
Chapter VII: Karma Yoga ................................................................... 47
Chapter VIII: Gunas ............................................................................ 53
Chapter IX: Role of Prakriti and Yoga .............................................. 69
Chapter X: Sufferings by Human Beings .......................................... 81
Chapter XI: Anger, Depression and Fear .......................................... 88
Chapter XII: Dharma ........................................................................... 97
Chapter XIII: Dharma in Practice .................................................... 105
Chapter XIV: Samadhi ...................................................................... 116
Chapter XV: Meditation Practice - Part of Dharma ...................... 121
Chapter XVI: Misconceptions and Mistaken Practices ................. 133
Chapter XVII: Realisation of Selflessness ...................................... 143
Chapter XVIII: Gyan ......................................................................... 152
Chapter XIX: Taking Refuge in Him ............................................... 164

## SECTION II: MEDITATION

Chapter XX: Need of Meditation ..................................................... 173

Chapter XXI: Obstacles in Meditation ............................................... 179

Chapter XXII: Control of Mind ......................................................... 184

Chapter XXIII: Position for Meditation ............................................ 189

Chapter XXIV: Reconciliation of Body and Mind ............................. 195

Chapter XXV: Inevitability of Death ................................................. 205

The Author ........................................................................................ 211

# Preface

Karma, Dharma and Meditation are the basic ingredients of Hindu way of life. These have been deliberated in upanishads and puranas culminating in Bhagwad Gita. Sri Krishna has in his discussion with Arjuna, who had given up arms in Mahabharata, when the armies of pandavas and kauravas were ready to fight, seeing that he will have to fight with his gurus, grandfather and brothers for the sake of attaining his kingdom, convinced him of his Dharma to fight.

There is a very thin line between Karma and Dharma but Sri Krishna has told that human being's Dharma is to follow the respective Varanashrama Dharma, which is his Karma and his further lives shall be determined according to those Karmas. Arjuna, being a Kshatriya, his Dharma was to fight. On Sri Krishna's convincing preaching, Arjuna got ready to fight and thus came about the battle named Mahabharata. Sri Krishna has told that one's duty is to observe one's Dharma and do the Karma leaving the result with God. So did Arjuna fight and Pandavas were victorious. The author has tried to illustrate in brief the same concept in this book with the intention that reading will imbibe the basic knowledge of philosophy of Karma and Dharma in the reader.

Meditation is a procedure to attain the aim of salvation. This exists in every religion in one form or the other. In Hindus it is 'Dhayana'. In Muslims, it is 'Namaz' and in Christians, it is a 'Prayer' in the Church. In this book, the way the meditation is performed, has been indicated illustrating the way of sitting, concentration and then attaining 'Dhayana'. Meditation stage is achieved with complete concentration in 'Brahma' after which one achieves the stage of 'Moksha', which is ultimate aim of human being. With the procedure of meditation illustrated in this book, one does start the meditation and this is the aim of writing this book.

**D.D Agarwal**

# List of Hindi Words with English Translation

| | |
|---|---|
| Adhisthan | Santum Santorum |
| Adhyatam | Spiritual |
| Agnihotra | Sacrefice of fire |
| Ahankara | Pride |
| Arjuna | Third in Pandavas |
| Asan | A mat to sit for meditation |
| Asatya | Non truthfulness |
| Bhagwad Gita | Surmans of Krishna to Arjuna |
| Brahamcharya | Studies Time |
| Brahma | The Creator |
| Brahman | Priest, teacher |
| Brahmanic, Upnisidic. Milieu | Upanishada as interpreted by brahamins |
| Brihadaranyak Upnishad | Name of an Upanishad |
| Brihaspati | A priest |
| Budhichita | Application of Brain and Mind |
| Budhiyoga | Intellectaul life |
| Chesta | Attempt |
| Chhandog Upanishad | Name of an Upanishad |
| Chitta | Mind |
| Daivya Sampada | Divine nature |
| Dharamshastras | Religious books |
| Dharitrastra | Father of Kaurvas |
| Dharma | Acting as per tenets of religion |
| Dwesh | Enmity |
| Grihasta | Creation and brought up of family |
| Gunas | Way of discharging duties |
| Gurukul | School |

| | |
|---|---|
| Gyan | Knowledge |
| Karamyoga | Full of action |
| Karana | Intrument through which action is held |
| Karma | Duty, Action |
| Karta | Actor |
| Karya | Job |
| Kshatriya | Rulers and fighters |
| Kurukshtra | Battle ground of Mahabharat |
| Manas | Mind |
| Manu | First man on the earth |
| Manusmriti | Code of basics of hindu religion |
| Neru | A priest |
| Nivaritti | Actionlessness |
| Parke | A priest |
| Prakriti | Nature |
| Pran | Life |
| Prarabdha | Fate |
| Rag | Affection |
| Rajo Guna | Discharge of duties involved in wotldly affairs |
| Ramayan | The book on Rama's life |
| Samadhi | Deep concentration |
| Sankhya | Way to control all parts of body |
| Sanskara | Way of action |
| Sanyas | Pearching while living in forest |
| Sat | Truthfulness |
| Satva Guna | Discharge of duties on truthfulness |
| Shankar | A priest |
| Shastras | Religious books |
| Shudra | Servers of the brahmins, Kshtriyas and Vaish |
| Tamas Guna | Discharge of duties in menial way |
| Tapa | Deep devotion |

| | |
|---|---|
| Upanishadas | Book containing details of topic of Vedas |
| Vaish | Traders and agriculturists |
| Vanprashtha | Leaving worldly life to adopt forest life |
| Varnasharam | Division of four casts and four stages of life |
| Vedic Religionists | Followers of Vdedic tenets |
| Vitesh | A priest |

# SECTION I: KARMA and DHARMA

# Chapter I

## Introduction

Karma is a Sanskrit word which strictly speaking means "action". But what follows from action is a result, a consequence, which is why we call it the law of cause and effect. All of us take this law for granted in our daily lives such as when we put the car key in ignition, we expect the car to operate, we push some keys of computer and we get the desired information and so on. The whole world operates according to cause and effect and there is direct relationship between these two. It is same with mind. Every thought we have, every word we say, every action we take, create a cause and over a period of time all these karmic causes ripen to become effect. Every moment constantly shapes our karmic destiny. The good thing about the law of karma is that we have it in our power to create the causes for whatever effects we wish. Many people think that karma equals fate or predestination and think that one does not have any power to change. This is a misunderstanding. It is we, who create our own karma and we can change it in a powerful dynamic way. We are creating thousands of such cases every day of our lives. But unless we have good mindfulness, we may not even be aware of it. So we see how important it is to subdue our minds to be fully present in each moment. It is not only the big thing we do that matters. We do not have to do anything as dramatic as defraud our employees or with a large cheque to a charity to create negative or positive karma. Both of these actions, like all others, begin as ideas in our minds, so that it is here, in our mind, that karma arises. We all tend to have habitual thoughts or attitudes, and we need to be very careful about these as often they build and have a cumulative effect which is immense. If we want to know how our life will be in future, we should look at how we think and act today. We are the sum total of the decisions we take or say our present condition is not something causeless nor is it something caused by chance. It is something we ourselves have steadily constructed through our series of past decisions and the actions of body, speech and mind that arose from them.

The aspect of karma is significant in revealing that we are the authors of our own future happiness or misery. Even in the most desperate circumstances, we still have the opportunity to create limitless positive or negative karmas. The small business owner going through bankruptcy, the middle-aged wife, whose husband leaves her for a young woman, even the forty something man struck down with a life-threatening illness – all these people still have a choice in the attitude they adopt, which will determine their future experiences. In karmic terms they create the causes for still further unhappiness in the future. By contrast, through ridding ourselves of our "we" focussed attitude, the most traumatising adversity can be faced with far greater equanimity than would otherwise be possible. Personal tragedy can actually be transformed to become a cause for limitless future happiness and we do not have to look far to find examples of people, who are able to rise above personal tragedy to help others. Therefore, karma is challenging subject because it turns upside down the idea that all our joys and despair arise from what happens in the world around us.

But it is ultimately the more-empowering psychology than the one most of us take for granted, because it offers us the chance to transform our whole experience of reality. All great men use the analogy of planting seeds, when talking about future. It is good analogy not only because of the direct association between cause and effect but because of the implied factors which come into play. Those factors may be described as "conditions". In order for a seed to germinate and grow to a healthy plant; it requires soil, moisture and sun-shine. Similarly, karma needs the right conditions if it is to ripen. In our quest to rearrange the external circumstances of our lives, we are quite frequently like a foreman, who lavishes the very best soil conditions and fertilisers on his land, installs a state of the art irrigation system and expectantly awaits an abundant crop even though he has failed to plant a single seed. At times the people do all the right things but whose ventures end not in wealth but in failure. It is because all the conditions may have been alright but without the karmic seeds in place, success was never even a possibility. Therefore, just as conditions alone will fail to yield a positive outcome, so too will seeds without appropriate conditions. Hence the seeds plus conditions is the approach we need to adopt in seeking karmic results. It is an approach which resonates with many people, on both the rational and intuitive levels. But even there, why is it that the most exclusive suburbs of the world, major cities are not populated entirely by our most generous, patient and ethical fellow citizens.

Sometimes bad things happen even to the good people. We know karmic farmers, who not only tend to conditions but are punctilious about planting seeds as well. An entrepreneur, who not only runs a thriving business but is also involved in several charities, sometimes nasty happens the entrepreneur's company is hit by a sales slump leaving him with a humiliating prospect of bankruptcy. Farmers' crops are wasted by unseasonal cycles and so on. Here we have to accept that mind stream seems to have existed since beginningless times and such happenings have to be seen as karma ripening in our mind stream, which is why there has been a sales slump or the seeds which gave fruit two times may have failed once or it can be attributed to our own destiny. Our karma is subject to constant change. Because our mind stream is dynamic so too are the karmic seeds being planted and those coming to fruition through appropriate conditions will change from moment to moment. For this we have to purify the negative karmas and cultivate boundless positive karmas. The inheritor of even the heaviest karmic debt has it within his power to achieve enlightenment within a single lifetime and for this we have to take responsibility for ourselves and for our destiny. Acceptance of the laws of causes and effects invariably has the most transformative effect on our lives and at times we come to realise that our own selfish interest lie in being altruistic. Just as the flowering of the lotus transcends the filth of the swamp, so too is it that those of us who normally think of only ourselves start to behave in a way that gives rise to outcomes far beyond our imagination.

For this it is in our own self-focussed best interest to maintain strict ethics, because in doing so we are maximising our own future happiness and peace of mind. The more mindful we become of our thoughts and behaviour, the more alert we will be to our thoughts and behaviour, the more alert we will be to the opportunities to cultivate causes for future positive effects. It is the life's curious paradoxes that the goals to which we have greatest attachment are most likely to escape us, while those we do not care so much about just fall into our laps. The important thing is that we should not care too much if we lose, we should always put the deals up rather than giving a damn and in course of time we shall be winners too. Most sentient beings have only the most limited opportunity to create positive karma and develop their minds. Their short lives characterised by fear and aggression, it is inevitable that the karma they create will be overwhelmingly negative. We, on the other hand, have limitless opportunities to create positive causes but how well do we fare? Looking at our actions of body, speech and mind on day-to-day basis, how much of what we do is a cause for positive or negative future effects? This precious life, one which only the tiniest proposition of sentient beings enjoy, presents us with a rare opportunity to break through altogether from the endless cycle of rebirth and suffering. It is up to us to make the most of it. If we do not, we shall be like a trader going to an island of jewels and returning home empty handed.

In the value of thought there is no more pervasive unifying structure than karma. It is the doctrine or law that ties action to result and creates a determinant link between an individual's status in this life and his fate in future lives. Because of karma ubiquity, the doctrine is not easily defined. The bare meaning of the term karma is action. But as a doctrine, karma encompasses a number of quasi-independent concepts viz. rebirths, consequence fruit and the valuation or ethicization of acts qualifying them as good or bad. The same person enjoys the fruit of the same sinful or meritorious acts in the next world in the same manner and to the same extent according to the manner and extent to which that act has been done by him in this world. Despite karmic dominance in those thoughts, a detailed knowledge of its history has always eluded the thinkers. The differently scholars encountered in seeing one karma's result may be attributed to some degree to the arcane nature of India's ancient textual tradition, the vast corpus known collectively as Vedas. At the outset, Vedic culture was situated in the North West corner of Indian sub-continent and had shed its overt connections to its Indo-Aryan part. Since the karma doctrine has no obvious clear antecedents in the earliest layers of the Vedic literature, some scholars have suggested that karma's origin lie outside the sphere of ancient Vedic culture. According to the Hindu philosophy of karma, nearly all primitive and pre-literate societies possess simple theories of birth, theories that through a simple transformation can evolve into a karmic eschatology. This transformation occurs with the introduction of a link between the nature of actions in one life to either a state of retribution or reward in the next life, a transformation that is referred to as the "ethicization", of the simple rebirth eschatology. The supposition that non Vedic stream made a significant contribution to the karma doctrine is likely correct. Moreover it opens up what may be the most significant question in undertaking the history of karma that is when and how the systematic ethicization of actions occurs.

# Chapter II

## Ethicisation of Actions

However, the ethicization of actions cannot be seen in the Brahmanic Upanisdic milieu. Still within the context of the ritual performance, the Brahmanic authors do distinguish between good and bad ritual acts and as in other ethical systems this valuation is based on the consequences of actions. A passage declares when the Agnihotra is being offered, what he does mistakenly, either by word or deed that cuts off his vigour, his own self or his children. In other words within the narrow confines of the Vedic ritual system, a rudimentary ethical system does indeed exist. The Hindu tradition has looked to the Vedas as a model of cultural prestige and the legitimizing force for all sorts of religious behaviour. Moreover, because these texts were created not by individual authors but represent the thoughts, directives and observations of communities of inspired sages as they were recorded over successive decades, they are not highly systemised. As a result as they now stand and have stood so far the Vedic texts contain multiple and sometimes contradictory teaching on the same subject but at the cover, Vedic traditions, and certain other values exist. Foremost are those relating to the acts of sacrifices despite the changes in the thought and practice that may have occurred of the Vedic texts composition and compilation, the core remains clearly discernible, the acts of sacrifice—though variously enacted and variously interpreted by the Vedic religionists – stands always at the culture of the Vedic tradition. Karma is the critical component of this core. In early texts, the term "karma" typically denotes the action or performance of the sacrificial ritual, a usage that is so common that the term "karma" is then synonymous with the Vedic rites. As subsequently reflected in the Upanisads, karma emerges as a doctrine that is in a formulation that has a definite and extensive meaning and is rectified above and beyond its ordinary connotation. To understand karma's history it is first necessary to examine these early doctrinal formulations, a point that leads back to the action of the Vedic sacrifice. The term "karman" appears frequently in the Vedic context. As such karma is not understood here as a doctrine but simply as a term denoting action in particular the action of the sacrificial rituals. However, with the presentation of Upanisads, karma is presented as a doctrine, one in particular that expresses the notion that actions in one life directly affect the condition of future life/lives. Brihadaranak Upanishad speaks about action (Karma) and one indeed becomes good or bad action and man becomes good by good actions and bad by bad actions. This passage appears to present the fundamental premise of the karma doctrine as it dominates the later Hindu thought that is that an individual attains a state of the death i.e. direct result of the ethical quality (good or bad) of his activities before death. Although the central idea presented here that "one becomes good by good actions and bad by bad actions" does evoke the later formulations of the karma doctrine, but the passage fails to explicate several key elements that would tie it with certainty to the later karma doctrine in particular the question of what constitutes "good" or "bad" action and what is the precise action of the individual's post death existence, stands unanswered here. Karma again appears in Brihadaranak Upanishad in discussion of the fate of the individual upon the event of his death, this denotes that the individual approaching death "becomes one" as the vital energies together enter the individual's heart and gathered in the heart these elements then depart through one of the body's orifices, an event signifying the end of the individual's emanate existence. At the moment, at what appears to be the bruise of the dissolution, the deeds (karma) and knowledge and memories take hold of him (the deceased). This taking hold of apparently leads to the acquisition of new body just as a goldsmith takes a piece of gold and turns it into another, so the self makes another new and more beautiful shape, like that of the ancestors, gods or other beings and how one gets and how one behaves so that one becomes as the doer of good to become good and doer of bad becomes bad. This mentions of the new body being acquired but does not mention about the rebirth specifically - a critical component of the later karma doctrine – but to some sort of other worldly after life existence. It only states that "that one together with his actions, he goes when his inner mind is attached and when he reaches that the end of his action (karma), which he did in this world here, then he comes back to this world back to action", but not every-one returns to this world, the man who does not desire, his breaths do not depart Brahma and he is as Brahma does. The intimation here that the individual on the basis of the deeds performed in life may be reborn in this world, or alternatively attains the world of Brahma, appears again in an extensive discussion found in another passage, which is repeated in Chhandogya Upanisad. The questions raised there are "How people when they die, go by different paths, how they return to this world, how the world beyond is not filled up even as more and more people continuously go there"? The answer is that the material of the offering of this last creation is the body of the deceased, from which, placed in the sacrificial fire, a "shining" or "radiant" man emerges. The radiant man follows one of the two paths – the path of the gods, which leads to final existence in the world of Brahma (those who retain it are said not to return) or the path of the fathers (Pitras), which leads to the moon and eventually to another birth in the world. The attainment of one or the other of these paths is based on the type (though significantly, not the quality – for example "good" or "bad") of activity performed before death. Whereas the one who meditates in the forests and possesses an understanding of the homology of the elements of cosmos and the elements of Vedic sacrificial fire attain the path of the gods; the one who sacrifices and gives gifts to the priests attains the path of the fathers. Through the flames of the cremation fires, the deceased individual is first transformed in to smoke and then successively joins with the various worlds and elements that make up the Vedic cosmos. Reaching finally the moon, the deceased individual becomes the food of the gods and when this comes to an end, the deceased individual passes in to the sky, then in to the wind, then in to the rain, then to the earth and rebirth in this world. Here the people, whose conduct is pleasant, can expect to enter a pleasant womb like that of a priest, warrior, a common man/woman but they who are of stinking conduct can expect to enter a stinking womb, that of a dog, pig or an outcast. Both passages refer to a third path, that of worm, insect and other small creatures that revolve ceaselessly through birth and death. Neither a type or action nor a quality of action is specified for the creatures that follow the third path. The question that now arises is why is the karma doctrine that is as it is presented in the Upanisads, a specific rule relating action or conduct to the condition of the after-life, grafted into this stock teachings? This question, however, cannot be broached without a clear understanding of the import of the teachings within the original context that is a milieu dominated by the ideology and performance of the Vedic sacrificial rituals. The sacrificer's death and rebirth in the sacrifice effected through the journey to and return from the other world, is a necessary element in the sacrificer's acquisition of the rewards of the sacrificial performance. Journeying to the other world, the sacrificer is said to become one with the world of the gods to whom the sacrifice is directed. The unification of the deity and man is further expressed in the notion that in the other world the sacrificer becomes the "food" of the gods, which suggests an element of trans-substantiation but also underlines the precarious nature of the journey to the other world. The sacrificer returns to this world utterly transformed by this experience, "reborn" in the sacrifice, he is now in a condition to acquire the sacrificial largesse, the results of his sacrificial work (Karma). The lifting process of sacrificing of journeying to end returning from the other world and of acquiring the sacrificial largesse ends with the sacrificer's death and the final sacrifice (antesti) as the cremation rite is known. Here the sacrificer's body forms the material of the offerings. The journey to the other world and the subsequent rebirth that was realised in symbolic terms within the ritual arena is, in the event of cremation, actualised in real terms and the sacrificer's experiences again at the end of his life time and these performances clearly affect the conditions attained in the sacrificer's final journey. The early formulations of the Upanisdic karma doctrine draw heavily on the Vedic ritual substratum. First and foremost, the mechanism of the sacrifice – that is the action of the ritual performance necessarily yields a corresponding result, that the sacrifice entails a journey to the other world and a return to this one and that through the sacrifice the sacrificer acquires a new birth and so too implicitly must die is a fundamental premise to the Upanisdic presentation of the karma doctrine. The Upanisdic confrontation with the sacrificer's real death – expressed clearly in the simple question asked of the fate of the individual that frame the early presentation of the karma doctrine – suggests just such a return to the "lived in world". Yet the mechanism of the sacrifice – the nearly automatic acquisition of the results of the sacrificial acts and the journey to and return from the other world through which the sacrifice is reborn and thus prepared to acquire these goods cannot be left behind. These elements re-emerge in the Upanisdic formulation of the karma doctrine, the principles of which are no longer linked to the action performed in the ritual world but are now extended outward to the lived-in world and so encompasses all acts.

The post –Upanisdic history of the karma doctrine is that of near universal pervasiveness; for at least implicitly karmas penetrate even the furthest corners of the Hindu thought. Here it stands along with a handful of other doctrines that, following the Upanisdic period, are consistently presented as presuppositions of Hindu thought such as the doctrine of an underlying ego element and its relationship to a cosmic ground of being Brahma, of illusion (Maya) and of liberation (Moksha). In the post-Upanisdic period karma means, quite simply, that actions lead inevitably to certain results and that their results are realised after death. These two components – the effectiveness of action and its realisation in a future birth – emerge from the pattern of ritual action deeply embedded in the doctrines of Vedic part, that is that an action performed in the work of the sacrifice necessarily generates a result and that death and rebirth - even if realised symbolically – are necessary pre-requisites to the realisation or acquisition of that result.

# Chapter III

## Relationship Between Actions, Death & Birth

This relationship between act, death, rebirth and consequences leads to the notion that the nature of the existence in to which the individual is reborn – whether measured by force (human or non-human) or by class (caste) - a non-indigenous and somewhat misleading substitute for the general indie tem literally birth or by circumstance (wealthy, poor and so on) or alternatively by no birth whatsoever – results directly from the deeds performed in a former life. Now lurking beneath the general depiction of karma is the question of what precisely is the nature of action; how is it constituted and how it is qualified? In Brahmanic Upanisad, actions are qualified on two basis, neither of which excludes the other, by nature of the actions, in and of itself, and by the way in which the action is actually performed. In the first instance actions are valued on the basis of general morality. For example murder may be considered in a general way as "bad" act and hence generates a bad result. A man who steals gold, drinks liquor, takes to the bad action or kills a priest, these four falls and also the fifth who follows them. On the other hand the actions that are good in general way such as feeding a guest or rewarding a priest for his work in undertaking sacrificial rituals, clearly leads to a good result. The values associated to the acts reflect general moves to values that cross cultural and chronological boundaries. Along with the notion of "good" or "bad" acts, exists the notion of placing a value of actions on the basis of how they are performed that is whether an action is performed correctly (good) or incorrectly (bad) corresponding to the established model of action. In the case of sacrifice, the model as prescribed in one of the divine provenance, whereas precise imitation – in symbolic, if not in actual terms – leads to rich rewards, whereas the actions of sacrifice are the only actions contemplated and the actions themselves are defined by their role in the actual performance, the question of the value of actions in and of themselves is not raised. The distinction between the two paths – one who meditates in forests and the one who sacrifices and gives gifts to priests - the first leads to the path of gods and freedom from rebirth and the later leading to the attainment of the path of fathers and rebirth in the world – described as simple alternatives, meditation in the forests leads the individual after death to Heaven path, the path of sun and eventually to a permanent sojourn in the world of Brahma (the path of gods) and sacrifice on the other hand leads the deceased to a path that carries to the moon and eventually back to rebirth in the world. But we cannot suggest which is better of the two. Those, who consider sacrifices and gifts to be the best, they know nothing better, having lived in joy in the Heaven after death enter again this inferior world. This denigration of sacrifice signals a profound change in the ancient Indian world view, leading eventually to the expression of a deep antipathy to the Vedic ritual tradition. This antipathy develops from the karma doctrines' success that actions inevitably generate results and that these results are an organic element in an unremitting process of rebirth, weighed heavily as a vast burden, if not sorrow on the Indian psyche. This position leads to a paralysis in all actions and numerous Indian traditions seem to have adopted this notion of seeking the cessation of all activity, a position that in practice leads to the dissolution of society, if not culture. But Hinduism does not abandon the activity for inactivity. It describes the path of inactivity to exemplify a "wrong path". Even the Upanisdic depreciation of sacrifice is not a call to turn to a life of a complete stasis, for meditation in forests is still a form of activity and it is an activity built on the framework of the ancient Vedic sacrifices in a contemplative, cognitive and interiorised fashion for the Upanishdic path of meditation takes the activity of the Vedic sacrifice and internalises it.

The traditional sacrificial format is an act of social cooperation with assorted priests working in consort, one priest chants the prayer, another performs certain ritual actions, yet another watches for errors, all at the behest of another actor, the patron who stands at the edge of the ritual arena but is also intimately identified with the victim, the focal point of the sacrifice. In this the patron is the body of the sacrifice and the officrants of the limbs. The sacrifice engenders its own peculiar set of problems regarding the benefits of sacrifice, for the deep involvement of priests, who actually perform the sacrifice and take its inherent danger upon themselves, suggests it is they and not the sacrificer, who should be the recipients of the sacrificial largesse. The resolution to this problem was found in the giving of gifts that closely approximate the offerings to the officiants, thereby allowing the sacrificer to "ransom" the benefits of the sacrifice for his use. Nevertheless, the problematic nature of the "Karmic web" created by the sacrifices (Traditional) format remains a troubling factor as reflected in a number of Brahmanic Upanisdic notions regarding the dispensation of an individual's merit and demerit after death that is that it is "eater" or giver to the gods and ancestors or it is passed on to the relatives he holds dear and to the ones he despises or it is given directly to the offspring.

Against this background, the Upanisdic representation of "meditation in the forests" as an acceptable, if not superior, alternative to the traditional sacrificial performances indicates a significant sociological and stereological shift in the ancient Hindu way of life because the meditation in forests is clearly a path of individual attainment, a point understood by the fact that it is undertaken beyond the pale of the ordinary social life of village or town. Although the model of action underlying meditation in the forests is still the sacrifice – albeit in an internalised form – the rigid social web necessary for the traditional sacrificial performances is collapsed and these circumstances are mirrored in the condition of the after-life. On one level, this collapse eliminates the need to dispense the sacrifices' consequences (in this world and after death) for just as the path of meditation is an individual path, so too the acquisition of its consequences, belong wholly to the individual. On another level, by removing themselves from normal social intercourse, those who follow this path remain even after death outside the ordinary world, accordingly, after death there is "no return" for them.

The practice to Yoga is the direct successor to "meditation in forests". The fundamental purpose of Yoga is the suppression of bodies and mind's involvement in the ordinary, everyday world of existence. To achieve this goal, the Yogin disciplines his mind and body using highly developed techniques of breath control, concentration and body postures. Through this discipline, the Yogin no longer confuses the "non-eternal with eternal" and eventually gains a state of "ultimate freedom" in which his inner being is liberated from all material existence.

Among the explicit concerns of those who follow this discipline is the breaking of the Karmic process. This process begins with desire and continues to build up through attachment to the things of the world. Acting on these desires creates good and bad results the realisation of which carries the individual through an unremitting cycle of births and rebirths. These notions clearly represent karma in a pejorative light, for it is the link between acts and results that keeps the actor in a state of nescience. Awareness, and with-it freedom from rebirth is won only when the cycle is broken. Nevertheless, the discipline of Yoga is not built on a model of inaction but on one of "right action", a path that leads ultimately to the cessation of action. Thus initially the Yogi adopts a set of percepts or restraints (Yama) that have broad moral implications: non-violence, truthfulness, not stealing, chastity and renunciation of the material objects. The purpose of these restraints is to push the individual to "good" and thus to generate "good karma" and since this is accomplished in the ordinary world of existence, the Yogin's awakening occurs while there is still a karmic residue, a state known as "liberated in this life" and when this residue is consumed, freedom from ordinary existence is won and no further rebirth occurs. For this the Yogin eventually must remove himself from the ordinary world of every day existence, engaging in a discipline that necessarily leaves aside all familial and socretal relationships as involvement in the ordinary world of every day existence necessarily means a return after death to the same world of existence.

The Hindu texts clearly reflect a clear awareness that the elevation of "meditation in the forests" and the path of Yoga which succeed it as a viable means of life lead to the demise of society, for they promote a way of life that nullifies an individual's need as well as ability to meet his social responsibilities from raising a family to undertaking the sort of labour – farming, trading, soldiering – that allows the society's continued existence. The Bhagwat Gita, perhaps, the most widely disseminated and certainly the single most influential Hindu text in India contains amongst its deeply layered teachings what is clearly a direct response to this problem. Here action is enjoined with the significant caveat that an individual should do the work ordained by his nature.

# Chapter IV

## Varanashrama System

This notion refers to Hindu ideology of "Varna" that is that individual possesses inherent qualities that constitute them into specific sort of social beings viz. Brahmin, Kshatriya, Vaisha and Shudra. Each Varna's people have been entrusted with the designated jobs pertaining to that Varna. For Brahmin it is teaching and learning, sacrificing for themselves and for others; protecting subjects, giving, having sacrifice performed, studying and remaining unaddicted to the sensory objects are for a Kshatriya and protecting livestocks, giving and having sacrifice, trade, agriculture, lending money are for Vaishas and the Lord assigned only one activity to a servant to serve these classes without resentment is for the Shudras. Each Varna having been assigned certain actions is either incumbent upon or prohibited to the members of each social class and these notions redefine the "Karma" doctrine for they place a value on actions in accord with the parameters set forth by the duties of each Varna. This means that killing an enemy is for a warrior a "good" act whereas for the people of other Varnas it is "bad" and so on.

For this purpose each person after preliminary studies, opts the profession he wants to adopt based on his capability, on which the birth had its say, and then he adopts that vocation for further studies. Since the choosing of the profession is based on individual's capacity and liking, he does not have any grudge against the people of other Varnas who too act as per their capability and Varna. Initially it was prescribed in Manusmiriti. Having set out the general theory of how actions in one life lead to the conditions of future life, Manusmiriti offers a detailed list of specific acts and their specific results. Here the underlying mechanism of the karma doctrine appears to be a concrete relationship between cause and effect, in essence the punishment fits the crime or a man reaps the appropriate fruit in a body that has the quality of mind in which he committed that act. The notion that the value of actions lies in the performance of class-specific duties, is deeply embedded in the teachings of Bhagwad Gita, which gives the interpretations of sacrifice, meditation, yoga and the relationship of the individual to the cosmic, the nature of the Godhead and of course the nature of action (Karma) and duty (Dharma).

The most significant divergence between the popular and textual renditions of the Karma doctrine is that in practice Hindu tends to see events – in particular those that contain elements of misfortune or are in some sense tragic – as being the karmic results of the deeds performed in this life time. Though on this level Hindus do not deny the connection between the karma and rebirth, they seemingly pay scant attention to it and seem to feel immediate responsibility only for offences committed in the present incarnation, offences for the past incarnation belonging to a rather remote kind of self although in its classical formulations the doctrine is always presented as linking actions performed in one life with consequences to be realised in future births. In Manusmiriti it is said that good conduct such as maintaining habits of cleanliness (Swachh) and showing respect to teachers and guests leads to longevity, progeny and wealth, whereas bad conduct results in illness or a short life. The determinative relationship here is between act and consequence in essence that of karma doctrine. The notion of transferring or sharing of karma is another peculiar aspect of karma doctrine like in case of fire in a village, the villagers perceive the fire to be the result of the sins of the village leader, although they also see the fire as retribution for the villagers' accumulated sins i.e. a group enactment of karma. Similarly transference of merit between family members recalls the Upanisdic notion that the deceased dispenses his good and bad deeds to his kin. In Puranas, the transfer of merit and demerit is represented with some regularity, the mistreatment of guests, for example is said to result in the guest taking the good karma of the host and giving his bad karma in return. A king, who unjustly taxes his subjects, acquires as a result their collective demerits. However, such a view appears inconsistent with the doctrine of karma viz. if a man's sin is inherited it cannot be fruit of his own actions but of others as well. In Ramayana, husband and wife only share the good or bad karma and other relations are excluded.

It is an admitted fact in all religions that God created the universe. Before the creation of the universe, the almighty God was alone. He then thought of creating the universe. For this purpose, he at first created earth, water, fire, air, and space necessary for the formation of any creature in the universe. Then he created the Tamsic, Rajsic and Satvic Gunas to be inculcated in the creatures as per their requirement and then the Maya to control the creatures and have a protocolic link between the creator and the creature. At first the almighty God created the small gods. They praised God and requested for being told what they could do in the job of creation of the universe by the almighty God. After creation of gods, the almighty created the creatures by assembling the above ingredients with pride, heart and parts of various gods and a part of Him too. Thus he created Atma in each creature as his part and also the God's initial incarnate with hands, feet, eyes, ears, mouth, tongue, heart, brain etc. with the three gunas – Sat, Raj and Tum. God then created Vedas, trees, plants, medicines, birds and animals, human beings, rishis, munis, gods etc. All these creations are actually the assembly of many atoms. In our Vedas, shastras and even Bhagwat, the word atom has been used, thousands of years back and this is defined as the minutest form of earth, which cannot be further divided and which has not come in to operation and not so far merged with other atoms is called atom. All things created by almighty in the universe are the assembly of atoms. This definition of atom is even accepted today without any dispute and the atomic power is the result of the atom having been put in to operation. The persons so created started fighting with each other as also they multiplied in to such proportion that they could not be accommodated in the universe. Brahma then created fire to burn them but when they were being annihilated by fire, Lord Shiva came in to being, who requested Brahma to stop burning and took charge of annihilating the creatures in a phased manner.

Then to stop the existing human beings from fighting within themselves Manu created what we call the institution of "Varnasharma", which is the basis of the Hindu philosophy and it is for the raja to ensure that these are followed by all persons. The people had been divided in to four Varnas – Brahmin, Kshatriya, Vaisha and Shudra. In the beginning there was no difference in the people of various Varnas and entire universe was Brahmin only. Later on due to the multiplicity of jobs, they got divided. Those who indulged in leisure and were warrior-like became Kshatriya and those who engaged themselves in agriculture, trade, industry, etc. became Vaishas and the remaining, who could not fit in any of the three, became Shudras and their job was to serve the people of all the three Varnas. In this way those who were well-versed in Vedas, Shastras, conducting yagyas etc. became Brahmins. Their job was to teach Dharma to the persons of all the Varnas. In fact it was after completing the initial studies at the Gurukul, one was required to opt for the vocation out of the four prescribed Varnas.

Those who were interested in studies and teaching opted to become Brahmin, and their further education was in that direction only. Those, who were interested in governance, fighting etc. opted to become Kshatriyas; those, who were interested in agriculture, trade etc., became Vaishas and the remaining became Shudras. Since the Varna was accepted according to one's capability and was 'as opted' by the incumbents, no one had any grouse against the people of other Varnas and everyone was supposed to be acting as per his Varna and his further study was also in that direction. Brahmin was said to have born from the mouth of Brahma. Therefore, he was the best in Varnas. Study of Vedas, performing yagyas, accepting donations, imparting education to his pupils was his job. Brahmins could not sell foodgrains as it would have amounted to his collecting more and more of foodgrains in donation and selling it. So he could accept foodgrains as per his requirement only. He is responsible for proper performance of all Dharmas.

Kshatriya is responsible for the upbringing of his subjects. He protects his people from internal criminals and external aggression. For this purpose he used to get the help of people of all Varnas. He had to maintain an army to fight with the enemies and his soldiers for internal peace. This required lot of expenditure to be incurred for which he used to collect one-sixth part of the agricultural products plus other cesses on industrial products etc. The Kshatriyas are also responsible to sit in judgement over the crimes committed by internal criminals. The duties of the raja being multi-faceted are enumerated as under:

1. He has to control his senses.

2. He has to employ armymen on borders, in forests, towns, villages, parks etc.

3. After proper verification, he should appoint intelligent, blind, dumb etc. as his spies and post them at various sensitive points, markets, and peoples gathering places and in foreign countries. They are supposed to keep the raja abreast of what had been happening in their beats.

4. He should depute spies on his ministers, friends and even sons.

5. The spies should keep a track of the spies sent by enemies in markets, tourist- centres, social functions, parks, dharamshalas and conferences.

6. In case he finds himself weak, then he should compromise with the enemy and when he is stronger then he must fight with the enemy.

7. He should generally avoid battles but if it is forced upon him, then he should face it with full strength.

8. Before attacking enemy, he should ascertain his strength.

9. He should deal with the enemy according to the policy of sam, dam, dand and bhed.

10. Raja is also supreme justice. He should take assistance of his advisers while hearing the petitioner and defendant.

11. He should have a minister to take account of goldmines, foodgrain markets, coasts and the income derived therefrom.

12. Intelligent Pandits, specialists should be granted gifts and awards.

13. He should construct roads, parks, gardens, foodgrain stores, ordnance depots, cantonments etc.

14. In case of doubt on the integrity of any servant or minister, it should be sorted out immediately.

15. He should not consult the fools and ladies.

16. He should ensure that the people of all Varnas follow their respective Varnashrama Dharmas.

The kingdom survives because of the efficient management by the raja taking his subjects as his children and protecting them from internal criminals and external aggression.

Vaishas are helpful in the day-to-day living of the people. They are responsible for doing agriculture, trade, setting up industries, bringing up cows etc. and entertaining guests and persons of other Varnas as per their capacity and capability.

The Shudras are meant mainly to serve the people of the other three Varnas to the best of their capabilities.

Like Varnas, there are four Ashramas also prescribed by Manu. These are Brahamcharya, Grihast, Vanprastha and Sanyasa. The people of all Varnas go to the Gurukul for education. From here only their Brahamcharya Ashrama starts. In Brahamcharya, the pupil reports to the Gurukul for education. He serves the guru. He brings Bhiksha, gives it to the guru, who sets apart the share of each pupil. Every one, irrespective of the Varna he has come from, is treated equally in the gurukul. After preliminary education, which is necessary for all, one is asked to select a Varna for himself. It means one is not governed by the Varna of his birth. The option of Varna is according to one's capacity and taste. If one wants to be well-versed in Vedas etc. and desires to teach, he becomes Brahmin and is given the further education to enable him to become a Brahmin. If one is interested in governance, war etc. he opts to become a Kshatriya and is taught the usage of armaments etc. Remember that the gurus in gurukul were apt to teach the faculty of each of his pupils' choice (Dronacharya was best Pandit and best warrior). If one had taste in agriculture, trade, industry etc. he became Vaisha and the one who did not fit in any of the above three, became Shudra.

After coming out of the Gurukul attaining the education of one's Varna, he joins Grihasta ashram. In this ashram, he marries himself, preferably with the girl of the same Varna. Then have children and finds some vocation to bring up the family. The Grihastha has to do yagya; he has to have control on all his senses; honour the guests and beggars. When the children come of age, he has to get them educated, settled in some vocation and arrange for their marriage. He has to live with one wife only; he has to keep the study of Vedas etc. and to follow the same. In Vanprastha, one leaves the house, either alone or with wife, if she intends to accompany him. There he has to pass his life as a mendicant. The provision of Vanprastha has been made with several purposes in view. Firstly, when a person is born, he has a duty towards parents, guru and God. He is, therefore, required to discharge the duty towards God to have the best end of life. Some people go to Vanprastha after Brahamcharya itself. But after Grihastha, one has to go. Secondly, when the sons come up of age, they want to manage the vocation of their father. The raja's son wants to become raja; the Vaisha'a sons want to control the family doings. So rather than the son asking for the same, it is better the father himself hands over the rajya/family business etc. to the sons otherwise some Aurangzeb would be born and he would capture the kingdom and imprison the father.

In Sanyas, one can come from Brahamcharya, Grihastha or Vanprastha. One becomes a complete hermit. He has no belongings and keeps wandering, teaching the Dharma. He does not stay for many days at one place. He lives on bhiksha and spends his life in meditation etc.

The above description of Varnas and Ashramas is as is provided generally. But as already indicated, the Varna was as adopted by the individual based on his capacity and capability. Therefore, if one, say a Shudra, reads Vedas etc. and becomes well-versed in that, he could become Brahmin. A Kshatriya could also become Brahmin as Viswamitra, although a Kshatriya, became a Brahmarishi and Parsuram, although a Brahmin, did the job of a Kshatriya and killed all Kshatriyas of the universe twenty-one times as the Kshatriyas at that time had started misappropriating the money collected from the public in leisures and pleasures without caring for the well-being of the subjects and without caring for their protection. There are, however, some jobs which the persons of all Varnas have to do. These are no rage, truth-speaking, proper distribution of wealth, be contented, be prepared to pardon, leading a pious life, no jealousy, leading a simple life and helping the infirms, reading Vedas and Shastras. Here the study of Vedas and Shastras has been prescribed for the people of all Varnas and not for the top three only. It was only subsequently devised that Shudras and ladies were not entitled to the same. The Brahmins were, however, required to be thorough in the knowledge of Vedas and Shastras as they had to teach the same to others. The Brahmins should also take alms but not ask for the same and also not have more than their requirements. Kshatriyas should give alms but not beg. He should perform yagyas but should not perform for others. He should read but should not teach;

should care for all the people; should impose punishment on criminals and face external aggression. Vaishas are to give alms; study Shastras and Vedas; perform yagyas; earn money in lawful ways; grazing and bearing of animals; trade; industry, bearing up Brahmins, Kshatriyas and shudras; payment of one-sixth of the products to Government exchequer. Shudras should not have wealth of their own and it is always under the master's ownership.

# Chapter V

## Arjuna's Misgivings

The people of all Varnas were obliged to do their karmas as per the requirement of their respective Varnas and non-observance of the same was considered as a social crime. What is the crime caused and why the work of the Varna had to be done has been discussed in the Bhagwad Gita in detail, when in Mahabharata battle, Arjuna refused to fight after seeing that he shall have to kill his gurus, brothers etc. and the gain shall be only a piece of land, he said that he would forego that land rather than be responsible for killing his closest people. Arjuna's words depict the despair with the realisation that his very individualised existence, even unattached to any objectivity and endowed with the highest virtues between himself and the happiness he seeks, he at the same time failed to understand how virtue can be in the way of one's happiness. Further, how could he be happy by killing his own relations?

Arjuna had left to him his own subtlest objective 'I' when he arrived at the centre of the two armies. He had himself drawn away from every other objectivity. The Pandavas tended towards subjectivity. The tendency to objectivity characterises the sons of

Dharitrashtra. But why, thought Arjuna, should he wish their destruction. His belief did not drive him to objectivity but conformed to the virtues he had developed. He thought that destroying them was to destroy and neglect virtue; it was to destroy those who did no harm and so it was a sin and that he could not be happy by destroying them. His karma at the moment was to fight as is the job of a Kshatriya but he was prepared to sacrifice his karma if it could save the killing by him of his kins, who with their intelligence overpowered by greed did not see the guilt of family destruction but he could not turn away from this sin as he saw the guilt of family destruction and in the destruction of family perished the immemorial family Dharma; in the perishing of Dharma, Adharma would overcome the whole family. In Adharma women become corrupt and in corrupt women a hybrid takes birth, which only takes to hell the family destroyers and extinguish the eternal caste Dharma and family Dharma, taking them only to hell. This entire exercise was to commit sins for the satisfaction of the greed and pleasures. In the situation, it would be better if the sons of Dharitrastra killed him unresisting and unarmed. He thus showed perfect unconcern as to the consequences to himself of his conduct in abstaining from fighting.

The preservation of the virtuous family influenced him in his conduct but the Kaurvas, the concentrated sanskaras as centred them, seemed as determined as ever in their objective tendency. They were influenced by Rajas Guna of Prakriti as they were not content with their present lot and were greedy to what the Rajas would secure to them. They, in their attachment to such objectivity and selfishly inclined, did not see or cared what injury they would do to the family as formed to the central 'I'. Kauravas in tending towards objectivity tended to break up the virtuous family, by which the family Dharma would begin to disappear with its members becoming immersed in the vices of objectivity; disharmony and conflict. The senses through the bodies are what bring the being in touch with the objectivity. His subjectivity is lost in the Tamas to which he became attached and thus becomes family destroyer, who in his selfish greed is turned to objectivity and by his conduct generate vices which overspread the family and cause confusion of castes. Arjuna started in search of happiness which he did not find in objectivity. He advanced towards subjectivity and arrived at subtlest objective "I" centred in Manas. Then the very first effect was bewilderment. He, therefore, thought that the battle was a sin resolved by his adherents which attempted the destruction of those who were his own in exchange for the greed for dominion and happiness. Arjuna, therefore, consistently preserved his attitude of perfect unselfishness and self-sacrifice as a real Mumuksha. Arjuna left the arms and sank in the chariot. This was against the principle of karma and the karma and Dharma of a Kshatriya, whose duty in the battle-field was to fight, kill his enemies and to take back his rightful dominion grasped by the enemies. This job had to be done by Krishna to put him on right track for fighting.

There is a thin line between the karma and Dharma as an act of karma according to one's karma becomes his Dharma as well. Now, therefore, the first problem was to bring him around to do his karma. He asked him to give up this mean endeavour and get up for doing his karma i.e. to fight. He asserted that the influence of that impurity had overcome him at the most critical moment i.e. when the armies of both sides had collected and the fighting had to start. He told Arjuna that his determination was "Unarya" like, inglorious and Swarga-closing. His action was "Unarya" to not to fight when his opponents were challenging him, it was inglorious as his going away from the battle-field will bring him inglory and also close his doors to go to Swarga, as only those go to Swarga, who discharge their prescribed karma. But Arjuna, still daunted by his misconception, argued for being a beggar rather than killing his guru and closest kins. He was not clear what he had to do and left it to Krishna to advise him as his guru, as in such a state of despair and indecision, one has to go to the guru only for guidance. Arjuna, being perfectly virtuous per se, with not the slightest trace of selfishness in his nature assured the guru that he was apt to be coached of his karma. Krishna started with the universal truth that those whom he did not want to kill were neither there before nor will they be there hereafter and even he, the rulers and all were by chance there. He said that he grieved for those who ought not to be grieved for and this is what Krishna proved to him. On the contrary he told that he saw their existence to be finished in fighting but in fact he himself, the kings and others gathered there for fighting had no break in their continuity of their existence as they were there and will continue to be there except that they may change their bodies. So in actuality they ever existed and if anything ceases to be, it is the body and not what indwells it. The contacts of senses verily are givers of pleasures and pain, they come and go and are impermanent, which had to be endured. So the existence, whatsoever, continues the same and then offers no ground for grief and of the everchanging of the bodies and Prakriti which accounts for and generates contacts producing harmony and disharmony and is constantly liable to change in the mutuality of relation and who feels no concern for and is not troubled by them attains to immortality. Therefore, "Astya" has not being and "Astya" has not non-being. It is "Sat" that the body changes but "Astya" has no being. Therefore, as every body is subject to such change and passes in to non-being, it is "Astya" and as such it never has being. On the contrary "Sat" is all and every where and it never passes into non-being, so what thus ever is and never ceases to be is not born nor does it ever die because birth means coming to being and death means passing into non-being. The existence is not eliminated by fire, water, air and is eternal, all pervading, stable, immortal and ancient. Therefore, the embodied (self) in the body of all is ever unslayable and one should not grieve for any being. Grief had over-powered Arjuna when he threw down his weapons, sank in his seat in chariot, having the idea of Adharma which he saw in fight and which was repugnant to his virtuous nature, had stayed his hand and made him abstain.

# Chapter VI

## Krishna's Advice

Krishna having shown the groundlessness of his grief comes to Arjuna's Dharma. As Kshatriya he should know no fear and for him abstaining from fight was a sin for fear of self. So fight for him was not a sin nor should he expect any selfish gain from non-fighting and expecting any gain therefrom would mean concern for objectivity and Tamas which was as much unkshatriya-like as abstaining from fighting. The fight was not sought by him but enforced by his opponents and such an unsought fight to a Kshatriya has for its immediate result the opening of the doors of Swarga if he engaged in it in right earnest with a proper spirit of unselfishness. The non-fighting would mean that:

1. He would fail in his Dharma which demanded in a Kshatriya non-attachment to Tamas or objectivity and freedom from fear.

2. His abstaining from fight meant nothing short of putting a check on his Rajas.

3. It was quite unkshatriya-like and degenerating for him.

4. He failed in his Dharma of a Kshatriya, tarnishing his glory and Swadharma.

5. Such a loss of glory was worse than death for a Kshatriya although he had been advancing to non-fighting because of the non-knowledge of the consequences of non-fighting.

6. Till the start of the battle Arjuna had been advancing towards subjectivity unselfishly and unconcerned for objectivity, he stood high in esteem and respect for Maharathis but the tinge of selfishness would only lower him in their esteem.

7. In the fight he might either fall or come out victorious. His fall would mean his incarnatioin coming to an end and getting salvation and his victory would mean the rule of universe which is the wish of any Kshatriya and would be in harmony with the whole universe.

8. There would be no loss of effort or disappointment and even a little of Dharma would save him from great fear.

He should, therefore, fight thinking it as his karma and Dharma as a Kshatriya renouncing his attachment to defeat or victory. He should not, therefore, care for the result, as with manas undisturbed in pain and devoid of any longing for pleasure and free from affection, fear and anger is called a muni.

One who completely withdraws the senses from the sense objects, his awareness is well-established. These actions lead one to Rajas ending with the destruction of self, first as agitating and then as coursing and differentiating and finally as coming in conflict on the plan of objectivity. The self centralised in Sattava, however, avoids all such consequences and his ultimate destruction by the conviction that whatever the agitating Rajas in association with him, whatever its course, whatever it encounters on the plan of objectivity i.e. Rajas in whatever form and howsoever modified which energises the self is centralised in Sattva always and takes its clue and trend from what is ordained with a view to maintaining the universal harmony to which the whole evolutionary course of which it forms a factor would even make it conform.

The attitude of karmayoga portrayed so far is marked by perfect unconcern for actions i.e. for the course of Prakriti. It is more the Prakriti that is having its course and generating actions than that the Yogi in performing them. Arjuna, however, imbued with the sense of "I-ness" and thus unable to realise existence independent of the limiting and energising Prakriti, could not understand the Yogi's not performing actions while the Prakriti is allowed its fullest play. He could not separate the energising Prakriti from what it energises. When Krishna said that action was inferior to Budhi Yoga and that in the latter only he should rest refuged, Arjuna understood him as recommending something which was not 'action'. His inaction he could not reconcile with his Prakriti having its play as what he understood was to be engaged in fight was action and if action was inferior to Budhi Yoga, then why should he be induced to action which is deemed cruel according to him and which he wanted to avoid. But at the same time Krishna recommended action in the form of fighting and in the same breath advised him to take refuge in Budhi Yoga. This is what he could not reconcile and wanted to be told clearly either of the two whichever would tend to his certain well-being. In Arjuna's opinion action i.e. Prakriti having its course and Budhi Yoga could not go together whereas Krishna advised him to take refuge in Budhi Yoga and at the same time asking him to fight, showed that they were not inconsistent and could go together. Therefore, Krishna had to dissuade him from the mistaken notion that his taking refuge in Budhi Yoga would enable him to avoid the cruel action of fighting which was of his liking. Krishna told that he spoke about two points of view to him to consider. These are Sankhya Yoga and Karama Yoga. One adopting the former is Budhi Yogi whereas the refuge in the later is Karamyogi. Sankhya Yoga consists in realising the Purusha that one is in essence as distinguished from Prakriti and the Karamyoga consists in one's avoiding being influenced by Prakriti which is the source of his bondage and misery.

Whether one's aim is the realisation of what he in essence is or the accomplishment of his freedom from the bondage and misery which got him his present individualised existence he cannot deny, and as an individualised being, he is in association with the individualised Prakriti. This same Prakriti energises him and generates actions as also limits and confines him. From this Prakriti proved all actions which he seems to be performing. Thus feeling no concern for his Prakriti and individualised being will evidently not concern himself with its course, much less with what it leads to and this applies equally to Sankhya as to the Karam Yogi. Then nothing binds or limits him and he attains to perfection. It is, however, not the presence of Prakriti or the being's association with it but his attachment to and identification with Prakriti that subjects him to its influence.

It is, therefore, not by non-undertaking of actions that one attains to actionlessness. In fact non-undertaking of actions means not letting the Prakriti in association with oneself have its course and thus generate actions. Thus it is through actions i.e. by letting the Prakriti have its course that a being attains to actionlessness. Arjuna's abstention from fighting meant his non-undertaking of action and as such it was neither actionlessness nor would it lead him to it and if he thought that such abstention was Budhi Yoga, he was much mistaken as Budhi Yoga did not mean that there should be no action or that a being should abstain from them but only that he should have no concern as to whether or what actions are generated by the energising Prakriti being left to its course. Arjuna was not being forced to action as he seemed to think but he was only told not to abstain and thus betray concern for the course of energising Prakriti. No being could remain without action any more than he could be individualised without Prakriti. Thus while a being could not even for a moment remain without actions, he could rest in Budhi yoga all the while.

Arjuna by his abstention strives that there shall be no action, which was impossible as actions would be there inspite of him because Prakriti would assert itself rather his attempt to abstain was in itself an action. He had to exert himself making Rajoguna play. Arjuna only wanted his organs to be held back from action because they tended to go when he did not want them to go. He might not be feeling any attachment for objectivity but he could not hold back Prakriti from its action and he is not the least concerned or troubled as to whether, how or where, did it go. He imparted no impulse to the senses nor felt any concern for the impressions they brought. What was this control of senses? These were neither restrained nor prevented from functioning nor did the person care where they went. There is nothing in the objectivity too where he wanted to go. It was thus not by self that the senses had to be controlled but it was by Manas that they had to be controlled and it is Manas only which determined the functioning of senses. The attitude of Karma Yoga thus consisted in letting the senses function as determined by Manas which controlled them and the self feeling no concern as to whether or how they functioned and this attitude was superior to the one in which the senses were restrained and more or less prevented from functioning.

# Chapter VII

## Karma Yoga

An ordinary man objects to the senses being let loose indiscriminately without regard to the harmony or disharmony, pleasure or pain, good or evil which they caused in their functioning. He only directed the senses towards virtue and drawing them away or restraining them from vices. This was exactly what Arjuna was doing when he restrained from fighting. Such a person, however, devoted to virtue has not quite ceased to be slave to his senses. So it is not the Karamyoga which was revealed to Arjuna but the development of virtue which any one could understand and felt devoted. He would have been advised not to think of and never to let his senses drive him to sin without minding what the self might have to sacrifice in the cause of virtue but Arjuna had passed that stage wherein virtue had to be developed and the senses had to be restrained from sin. The Guru thus explained to him the nature of what he knew as his self. However, virtuous, it was something individualised and associated to the three Gunas imbued Prakriti. The Prakriti by virtue of its Rajas Guna ever tended towards objectivity from which he had been all the while drawing himself away. The Prakriti thus left to its course towards objectivity, came in conflict with other coursing in objectivity. This conflict was the fight which came unsought to a Kshatriya and which was recommended by Krishna to Arjuna. This course of energising Prakriti was determined by the individualising mould, the Manas, was the functioning of the senses controlled by the manas and action was its result.

Karma Yoga, therefore, did not defend all sorts of vices and evils when it advocated leaving the senses to function as best as they could. The time for its revelation and adoption, however, comes when every vice had been eradicated and the being had grown perfectly virtuous and incapable of any vice even in thought. Such a being had passed the stage when the senses were required to be restrained. To such a person only the Karama Yoga as revealed by Gita had only to be recommended and revealed. The individual self when he passed beyond his individualising manas is selfless. He is no more conscious of or imbued with the sense of "I-ness" than in any individual cell in a being's body. The cells do not cease to function as everybody could see for himself. In every action of his, there was some individualised existence, some cell of his body that is functioning and such functioning conformed to the energising Prakriti from which it derived its own energy and had no selfish interest to serve. Therefore, there were not only actions but they were more extensive in relation to the Karma Yogi and are more in conformity with the universal harmony. The Karma Yogi did act unconcernedly and unconsciously, leaving his Prakriti to its course as did the Jivatma in letting the vital energy function among the cells rather more in such functioning is the proof of existence of them both. Arjuna had perfected his lower self and for his further progress his sense of "I" had to go, in other words he must be a Karma Yogi and this is what Krishna had recommended to him. In abstaining from fighting Arjuna clinged to his "I" but it would have been alright if Arjuna felt happy and perfect in the position he had attained but the fact was that he felt unhappy and despaired of the happiness he was in search of.

Hence Krishna revealed to him the path he sought i.e. the path of performance, action which verily was superior to non-action and this was the purpose of his body incarnation. Budhi Yoga, though superior to action, was not inconsistent with it and would not justify Arjuna's abstention from fight or the state of inaction, which was only holding back his Prakriti from its course. To such inaction, action was definitely superior.

Above the Prakriti, Budhi Yoga and Karam Yoga, there is something like 'Prarabdha' for that incarnation. Every incarnation in the body is an opportunity offered to the soul to secure exhaustion of the Prarabdha which served as his bondage and to realise his essential nature and attain to perfection. The incarnatioin thus has double purpose to serve – first it is intended and ordained to serve and contribute to the maintenance of the harmony of the universal course of evolution and secondly it serves as an opportunity to the individual to ensure his well-being and liberation. Arjuna decided in abstaining from fight and favoured inaction but the incarnation impulse with which it had come was not allowed to conform and contribute to the universal harmony, nor its course determined by the universal course of evolution. He thus tried to thwart the first purpose. Also Arjuna's abstention meant preventing the exhaustion of his Prarabdha and generating fresh sanskaras for future bondage. He thus failed to avail himself of the opportunity for liberation offered to him in being sent out to incarnation and made it only a means for future bondage and so he thwarted the second purpose too. Action thus fulfilled the purpose of one's incarnation and inaction always defeated it. Action, therefore, was superior to inaction. This Loka was the plane of humanity with the development of Manas which gave to the being the power to discriminate between right and wrong. To attain this, the being that had attained the position of even a god, must incarnate on the plane of humanity and affect his progress further till he attained the Supreme Goal. Action thus binds the human being and to remove this bondage is his aim by doing action and action other than that for the sake of Yajna is the cause of bondage to a human being on the plane of humanity. Also Yajna is the worship or service and its every essence is action but every action is not Yajna. Worship or service meant surrender of one's self to the object of his devotion. Krishna, therefore, asked Arjuna to feel unattached, perform action for the sake of sacred

Yajna but Arjuna still abstains and this is his inaction. Such prevention on his part was not Yajna because it was nothing short of selfish interference in the course of Prakriti. Such inaction or absenteeism was cause of his bondage while action would or would not be so. Thus action was superior to inaction. As such Arjuna was not forced to action but was only dissuaded from abstaining from action which was not Yajna and was, therefore, because of his bondage, which was not desirable at all.

A being cannot remain without action for even a moment even Arjuna's abstention meant exertion on his part and was, therefore, action. It is, however, worse than inaction as it defeated the purpose of his incarnation and generated fresh sanskaras for his bondage and certainly could not be called Yajna. Now since action was inevitable, then why not allow it to take the form of Yajna so that he could avoid bondage effect on himself and Yajna as such was the command of the almighty for every creature. Any abstention from the Yajna marred all progress, disturbed universal harmony and could not even fulfil the will. Now let us see what the aim of the being was. It might be unalloyed happiness, realisation of truth, freedom from bondage and attainment of perfection and in all these he needed the unity of subjectivity away from the limiting, obscuring and agitating objectivity. Every being, from the subtlest to the greatest, had his energy and intelligence differentiated and confused by the ever-restless Rajas and limiting by the Tamas which gave him the form and from which he avoided or say he meant freedom from the three Guna Prakriti which is impossible to attain. It is, therefore, necessary to develop Rajas to its fullest extent so that Tamas did not confine it. This required action and not abstention. From Rajas only the being attained the essence, from all possibility of disharmony with no binding of Tamas, leading to the supreme goal of secured aim of life, the truth, peace, bliss and perfection. Once the being has overcome his attachment for Tamas, he refrained from all attempts to confine him to Rajas, generating action which meant growth, development and rise of god in the being as every modification of the differentiating Rajas had its corresponding god and gods playing within him helped him in their turn in the Yajna in which he was engaged and whereby he could satisfy and nourish them and attain the supreme goal and enjoyment which was due to the harmony created by gods. Arjuna's abstention meant preventing the energising Prakriti from having its course. His conduct is not Yajna. He is not for partaking of what the Yajna brings to him as his share of its remains but he would cook himself i.e. determine what should or should not fall to his share. He attached himself to objectivity and disturbed universal harmony, thereby sinning against himself and others and whatever his enjoyments might be they all would not be unattended with sin.

# Chapter VIII

## Gunas

The Beings are produced from food; the food is formed by rain; rain is generated from Yajna and Yajna is born from karma, karma is produced from Brahma; Brahma springs from the imperishable. Therefore, the all-pervading Brahma ever rests in Yajna. It is, however, the wheel revolves and whoever does not follow he is of sinful life and feels enjoyment in senses, lives in vain. Every being is made of five elements. These five elements mould the being as an embodied existence and nourish and strengthen it by making good the wear and tear which the body undergoes. Krishna rises with individual existence as the subtlest Ahankara where the Prakriti manifests with its three Gunas. It is the individualised existence that the karma or the energising Prakriti energises. This subtlest individualised existence is centralised in Sattava or Brahma. This Brahma from which proceeds and rises all possible action corresponds to the first and subtlest manifestation the Shabda Brahma, the universal being, the Omkara, as the root and essence of Vedas as also to the Jivatma, moulded in its subtlest sanskara and comes to manifestation from its seed form.

From Brahma starts the energising Rajas or karma. Its particular modification coursing towards objectivity is the Yajna which is but a form of karma and has as much Brahma underlying it as the karma itself. From Yajna is generated Parjanya, which is karma still further modified as individualised vibration which being essentially karma have Brahma undulying them. This all pervading Brahma rests ever established in Yajna and the whole universe being one grand Yajna, Brahma pervades it. The being's power to act and the energy the body exhibits, have their source in the sanskara. The being's sanskara is the resultant of his attachments in the past for the energising Prakriti for its harmonies and disharmonies and for certain forms on the plane of objectivity. The sanskaras as karma thus generate actions of the objective being and these actions in their turn stamp their influence on the sanskara. Every being being a link in the revolving chain of universe helps or tenders its progress according as it conforms to or not to the universal harmony. One who interfered in the ordained course of his Prakriti, fails to avail himself of the opportunity offered to him for freeing himself from his bondage which he more or less perpetuated and further disturbed the universal harmony and retarded the progress of the revolving wheel. Such a person lived in the universe in vain because his life that would have been utilised for ensuring his freedom and for helping others was lived to perpetuate his bondage and harm others. This is what Arjuna would be doing in abstaining from fighting which was his karma. He would, therefore, be defeating the purpose of his life. Further, the man delighting in the self satisfied with the self and content in self only, his actions did not exist. No interest of his is to be served by action performed or by actions unperformed nor is there any interest in his depending on any of the beings. Therefore, unattached one should constantly perform his actions which ought to be performed and by performing such actions one attains the supreme. But the man delighting in self only, satisfied with the self and content in self only, his action does not exist as therein there is no action he ought to do. His no interest is to be served by such an action if performed nor any by his actions unperformed nor is there any interest of his depending on any of the beings. Therefore, unattached one should perform actions which ought to be performed i.e. the man unattached verily performing action attains the supreme.

But by such actions a being might not feel delighted in the senses he might also not be attached to the harmonies and disharmonies of his energising Prakriti playing towards and in the objectivity. On the contrary, he may rest satisfied in the self and will be content in self only if viewed independently of the energising Prakriti in association with him. Certainly such was not the attitude of Arjuna in abstaining from fighting. He centred his interest not in the subjective self but in what Prakriti affected. Arjuna thus found delight in the senses and disturbed the universal harmony by his abstention and as such would be defeating the purpose of his life.

Therefore, he was confused in what he ought to do and what not to do. In such a situation one should do actions which his Prakriti left to itself ought to be generated in conformity to universal harmony and these are what had been ordained.

These are what he ought to allow not because he had interest in them or that they might secure him to anything but simply because his Prakriti must fulfil its destiny, whatever it be as allowing such actions unconcerned and unattached, one attains to the supreme. Actions do cause bondage to one who is attached to them but still one cannot stop them. Krishna repeatedly warned Arjuna against his being attached to them and since one cannot remain without doing any action, he must not feel attached to action. In other words it should be for the sake of Yajna. Janak had attained perfection through non-attached actions. Therefore, it is not that these actions lead to perfection but only their being allowed was not a bar to one's attaining to it and further that their being not allowed by trying to stop the course of the energising Prakriti actually kept one away from attaining perfection. One should, however, keep in mind that whatever an exalted being does, others below him imitate it and are guided by it. Thus everyone to whom his influence reached and who took him as his guide would be adding to the disharmony by following his example. He, therefore, must act even if he had attained to perfection because the universal harmony demands it. Arjuna should not selfishly act but he should at the same time not abstain from action and thus defeat the purpose of the universe for which the Lord himself acted. It was only selfish attachment to action that was wrong but the action was must for the universal harmony but should never attach to action. If unknowingly one attaches the acts to actions so the wise men should act unattached for the well-being of the Lokas. Therefore, the wise men should not unsettle the Budhi of the ignorant, who are attached to actions and should cause all actions to be regarded with favour at the same time he himself be harmonised and cooperating.

Through the Gunas of Prakriti actions are being performed. The Prakriti constitutes the body of the self but he is Prakriti as indwelling it, he is the embodied being. In the functioning of energised Rajas Guna of prakriti, he is an actor associated with Prakriti. But such association never meant that he should necessarily be deluded. So one knows himself that being distinct from individualising Prakriti means he is free from Ahankar or "I-ness". He knows himself as to what he in essence is, independent of Prakriti which has become associated with him and thus did not attribute to himself the actions. Karma is the outcome of the Prakriti so differentiating as it plays. In these differentiations of Guna and karmas, it is the Gunas playing among the Gunas. He does not, therefore, identify himself the indweller with the Prakriti he indwells – the Prakriti wherein he obtained the differentiations of the Gunas and karmas with the interplay of its Gunas. Such a person does not attach himself to the Gunas or to the actions which characterise Prakriti. One should not, therefore, abstain and allow actions to take place. The Prakriti should be left to its course and Rajas would be allowed free play. So there shall be actions but does not have to mind whatever they be. He should, therefore, fight as such an attitude was one of the Budhi Yoga or Karma Yoga as recommended by Krishna. The wheel of Sansara revolves like this – the subjective determines the objective and the objective influences the subjective and every one is a link in this chain. The incarnation of a person meant that the energy with which he had been endowed was wanted by and for the universal harmony.

This energy had been generated by him by the sanskaras in the past and in determining his incarnation, they are intended to be utilised for the furtherance of the progress of the universe, while giving him an opportunity to ensure his liberation from what constituted his bondage. He directed his action to minister to his self and is regardless of the consequences of his conduct to the revolving wheel of the Sansara, which he did not follow and to which he did not conform. That is what Arjuna would be doing in abstaining from fight by displaying attachment to objectivity and delighting in the functioning of his senses, perpetuating his bondage and disturbing the universal harmony. But the man delighted in the self only, satisfied with the self and contended in self only his action did not exist as there was no action he ought to do. He only thought that no interest of his was thereby served by action performed nor any by action unperformed, nor was there any interest of his depending on any of the beings. Therefore, unattached, he should constantly perform his actions which ought to be performed i.e. the man attached verily performing actions attained the Supreme.

Further, actions are generated by the energising Prakriti and resting content in the self he had no interest in the actions which Prakriti might generate or in those which it might not. This would only be defeating the purpose of his life. On the contrary, allowing such actions unconcerned and unattached, one attained the Supreme because every such action broke the bond that bound him by exhausting his Prarabdha and he remaining constantly unattached to objectivity generated no new sanskaras to bind him in future. It was through actions only that Janaka and others had attained to perfection. However, his abstaining from fighting would set a bad example for the people he led as they follow what the leader did. Besides denying himself perfection which he might sacrifice he would be by his abstention disturbing the universal harmony and this more or less injured the welfare of the Lokas which he thought he served as even the welfare of Lokas required him to fight which was his action as Kshatriya otherwise he would fail in the part that is allotted to him in its evolution and progress. If he sought perfection, he had to act and if he did not care for perfection or thinks he had attained it, even then he had to act for the universal harmony otherwise it would amount to selfish attachment to action which was wrong and not action itself. He, therefore, had to act and act without attachment. It was for the ignorant only to act duly attached to actions and the wise should act unattached for the purpose of welfare of Lokas. The wise men, therefore, should cause all actions to be regarded with favour himself harmonised and cooperating without caring for the attachment to actions of the unwise ones and set good example for being followed by the Lokas.

So the Gunas of Prakriti were being performed in which Prakriti constituted the body of the self. The self, therefore, indwells in Prakriti but is not Prakriti itself. In such a situation he speaks of "I" and is then said to be affected with Ahankar and deluded. He then identified himself with the individualised Prakriti and in the functioning of the energised Rajas Guna of Prakriti he treated himself as an actor. Here the self is deluded with "I-ness" that is why he believed himself as an actor and the one who considered himself as being distinct from the individualising Prakriti is free from Ahankar or the "I-ness".

He considered himself as what in essence is independent of Prakriti which became associated with him and thus did not attribute the actions to him. These he knew as springing not from him but from the Prakriti which he was not. Karma is the outcome of the Prakriti differentiating itself as it played.

In these differentiations of Gunas and Karmas it was, therefore, the Gunas which played among the Gunas. The knower, therefore, did not identify himself the indweller with the Prakriti he indwells and when the Prakriti obtained the differentiation of the Gunas and the karmas with the interplay of his Gunas. Such an aware person did not attach himself with the Gunas or to the actions which characterised Prakriti. Krishna meant to convey to Arjuna that he should not identify himself with Prakriti which his self indwelt. He did not do Gunas or karmas and should not, therefore, attach himself to nor appropriate the karmas which, therefore, he should neither advance nor avoid as he did when he abstained from fighting. Rather than abstaining, he only had to act in that he only had to rest intent on the underlying and indwelling self and disregard the Prakriti which formed his body; Prakriti being left to its own course. Rajas too would be allowed free play and should not mind for the actions whatever they might be. Thus calm and serene himself, he should let his Prakriti have its course i.e. he should resort to fighting. Therefore, it was not that by non-undertaking of any actions could one attain to actionlessness as none could even for a moment remain without action; that everyone was helplessly driven to action by the Prakriti born Gunas; that all restraint of senses while thinking of the objects was worse than useless and wrong; that Karma Yoga with non-attachment when senses were not prevented from functioning nor goaded to action but all left to be controlled by the Manas of which they are the differentiations, was superior to the restraint of senses; that allowing restraint actions to be performed was better than abstention or preventing action or inaction, which defeated the very purpose of one's incarnation, that action for the sake of Yajna should be performed unattached as they were never the cause of one's bondage; that Yajna was ordained and enjoyed by the Lord of Creation Himself when he evolved universe and the Yajna only depended its propagation and progress and the welfare of beings; that one's partaking of only the remains of Yajna attached himself to no sin, but on the other hand freed himself from all sins; that engaged in Yajna, one always contributed and conformed to universal harmony, and failing therein and delighting in the senses, he committed sins and lived in vain; that apart from his well-being and interest, one was called to action in the interest of the universe as a whole; that it was not that the unwise only should act and that the wise should not act; but it was only that the former acted from selfish attachment which the latter did in the interest of the universe at large; that it was Prakriti that generated action and that the self deluded with "I-ness" only posed as an actor; that the knower of the Truth, thinking that actions meant only the inter- play of the Gunas, was not attached to them; that it was the deluded one only that was attached to action; and that what was necessary was not inaction or abstention which misled the universe, but intentness on the underlying self with perfect unconcern for the Prakriti which was left to itself and would generate actions, which the being rested free from all "mine-ness" expecting nothing from the resulting actions.

Such a doctrine laid by Krishna did not allow or encourage action, but it condemned abstention or inaction. The essence of Karmayoga is to let the Prakriti have its course with perfect unconcern. The wise ought to do nothing less; the Prakriti thus having its course differentiated and met with harmony as also disharmony from the objectivity to which it tended and wherein it functioned.

Thus every being was supposed to do action discarding 'Rag' and 'Dwesh' as they were his enemies rather than actions. In the situation one should perform "Swadharma". For being Swadharma is the tendency of his incarnation impulse, of the mould of Prakriti that had become associated with him as his Prarabdha and whatever action it generated was the being's own Dharma and that was what he ought to do. That only was the purpose of his incarnation and allowing it he would be always contributing to universal harmony. Swadharma, therefore, had to be followed without thinking what the Swadharma might be, high or low, it was sufficient that it was his Swadharma and the being did not do anything wrong in following the same because it meant leaving Prakriti to its course, whatever it was. Swadharma, even if it be low, was better than following the Dharma of another, however, well the execution, and even though it might be high. The latter only meant not following or allowing what had been ordained in the moulding of his incarnation impulse, and diverting it to something for which it had not been intended. Even meeting death in sticking to one's Swadharma was better than Dharma of another which was full of danger. Arjuna, Krishna says, would be committing sin in abstaining from fight. The Prakriti does not drive one to sin and if at all it drives one to anything it will be only to Swadharma, which is not a sin.

Krishna advises him that it is desire (Kama), it is anger (Krodha), begotten of Rajas Guna, all consuming, all polluting. Therefore, these are the staunch enemies of the person. As fire is enveloped by smoke and mirror is faded by dirt and amnion envelops the foetus, so by Kama is enveloped the entire universe. His 'Gyan' is enveloped by Kama. Then Kama is the constant enemy and it is insatiable and it is always aflame. It is these Kama and Krodha only which are responsible for the sins being committed. The energising Rajas, while it helped evolution at the same time it destroys what it evolves. This destruction means the energising Rajas liberating itself from the Tamas which confirmed and moulded it. The being, with form thus destroyed, is reduced to the energising Rajas of which he or it was a mould. It is to the being as the fire is to the grosser elements which it consumes and devours. It is all polluting being the root of all sins and is the source of the beings' bondage and misery. Arjuna, by abstaining, wanted to avoid sin only as his energising Prakriti in its course threatened destruction of some whom he wished to continue and live. In thus wishing continuance of something which his energising Prakriti encountered and threatened with destruction, he yielded to Kama only. He might not have wished their continuance but at the same time did not want to be the cause of this destruction. This only justified his not driving his Prakriti but not his abstention or diverting it from its course. He would thus not let his Prakriti have its course and therein failed in his Dharma as well.

As Budhi, Manas or senses or as the energising Prakriti playing in them, Kama enveloped the existence of Sattva centralised in them. Budhi enveloped the centralised existence as smoke enveloped fire. Subsequently it is the Sanskara of the being coursing as Vasanas, which leave the self as smoke leaves fire and the purer the self, the finer, subtler and more intensely vibrating the Budhi, till all agitation ceased and then appeared only the glorious self all around.

Kama is like the dirt clouding and covering the mirror. It ranged from a fine film to a more or less deep layer affecting the transparency of the mirror. The mirror being Sattvik, and perfectly transparent, wherein rested the centralised being's self. The Tamas formed the film which had to be rubbed off required sacrificing the "I-ness" and it is the Kama that made him cling to the "I-ness" and it is Kama that prevented him from fighting. Therefore, the removal of Kama i.e. "I-ness" was not a sin and it was the Kama whose removal would encourage him to resort to fighting. Thus in one form or the other the Kama enveloped the whole universe and whoever yielded to it is forcibly driven to sin. It dislodged the being from the central Sattva and according to its degree of grossness it agitated and confused clouds and covers or destroyed his knowledge till he lost himself in the gross objectivity with which he identified himself. It obscured Gyan and was thus a constant foe of the Gyani and subjected the being who yielded to its influence to a succession of never ending birth and death.

The senses, the Manas and the Budhi are, as already explained, the seats of Kama as including the entire range of the course of the energising Rajas. These affected the Gyan centralised in Sattava, causing confusion, obscuration and disappearance in the objectivity and deluded the indweller who became attached to Kama which played therein. Thus in one form or the other Kama envelopes the whole universe and whosoever yields to it is forcibly driven to sin dislodging the being from Sattava and agitates and destroys his knowledge till he loses himself in the gross objectivity with which he identified himself. It covers and obscures Gyan and the more one yields to it and meets its demands the more it asks and stronger it grows. It thus subjects the being who yielded to its influence to a succession of never ending birth and death. The senses, the Manas, the Budhi are said to be its seat and by these it bewilders the dweller in the body enveloping knowledge. Therefore, it was necessary to first control the senses, which cause sins and destroy the Gyan and Vigyan. Thus beyond the senses is the Manas, beyond Manas is the Budhi and what is beyond Budhi is He, the indweller. Thus knowing him beyond Budhi and well steadying the self by self he should slay the enemy in the form of

Kama though it was difficult to overcome. But if this was done, then he would overpower his enemy, the Kama. This was the only way to slay Kama which was otherwise unconquerable. Arjuna abstained through his concern for his senses functioning towards objectivity, but apart from such concern, such abstention and forcible control of Kama was of no avail in slaying it. The only possible way out was to settle oneself in the self-centralised in Sattava beyond the Budhi and thus leave the energising Prakriti to itself and allow action which it might generate.

Those who desire success in this universe, they worship gods and success is attained born of actions and in accordance with the differentiation of Gunas and action the four Varnas (Brahmin, Kshatriya, Vaishya and Shudras) have been created. God is not concerned with what action the individual takes, nor is anyone bound by those actions so far as God is concerned. It is the individual who undertakes actions as per Gunas and Varnas. Those who surrender themselves to God, they do not feel concerned with objectivity. Such people are also not concerned whether their actions succeeded or failed, but there are others who desire success in actions.

They are devoted or are worshippers of one of the gods on the plane of manifestation. Such a worship demanded sacrifice and self-denial. For humanity, therefore, action born Sidhi or success in action is specially attainable without ceasing to be human but nothing that he sacrificed touched his own self whose interest only he advanced. Such a nature and such action characterised the Sattava being whose Varna is Brahmin. Another may have his Sattava dominated over by Rajas and would brook no opposition to his energy and power. Such a nature and such actions characterised the Kshatriya Varna which was Sattavik-Rajas. But when Tamas dominated over Rajas and Sattava, the being is attached to some form. Therein he differed from the Kshatriya, who tolerated no limits of form to his Rajas. Such is the Vaishya in Varna which is Rajasic-Tamas. Further, when the dominating Tamas overpowered Rajas, the being being averse to all progress which meant sacrifice of the tamas which rules. Such a person is of Shudra Varna. Now such persons of each of the four Varnas are the four natures or Varnas which characterised humanity, and have thus respective actions. He does not go beyond the Varna and his own self be perfected but did not sacrifice. Such a being even in his perfection is chained to Prakriti and is action bound and so is the god he is devoted to. Objectively only is his sphere of action with his inherit fruits. Now what is action (karma) and what is inaction, even the wise are deluded. Such karma for the persons of various Varnas was free from evil but from the karma verily, it is to be understood from the stand point of Vikarma (improper action) and Akarma (inaction).

# Chapter IX

## Role of Prakriti and Yoga

Who saw inaction in action and action in inaction he is wise, he has harmonised and has performed all actions, his undertakings are all devoid of desire of action singed by the fire of knowledge and having abandoned attachment to the fruit of actions, ever content, independent, even though engaged in action, he verily was not doing anything. Further, expecting nothing, the self, with Chitta controlled and had abandoned all his possessions even performing action which was purely bodily he was not polluted by sins. Such a person is satisfied with whatever came unsought, free from the pains of opposites, without any envy, balanced in success and failure, even though acting he is not bound and of one in whom attachment was dead, who was free, where Chitta was established in knowledge and who acted for the sake of Yajna, all his actions dissolved away.

Here one thing is common and that is that the Prakriti is allowed its course without any interference on the part of the self under any circumstance whatsoever. In the four attitudes he respectively styled their association, rid free, with Chitta resting in Gyan and

Yajna performing. Any one of these attitudes was unattended with karma but karma in each, after leaving the being, whose sanskara it formed totally disappeared in the universal energy and never appeared as the being's sanskara. Arjuna abstained from fight holding back his Prakriti from its course he believed it inaction although it was not inaction. It was self in action i.e. with self selfishly determining what action there should be instead if allowing the Prakriti to determine as ordained. It was also Vikarma (improper action) as every such action invariably was. It was not karma in Akarma (inaction) in which the self remained perfectly passive and Prakriti was left to generate actions as ordained and all karmas generated Gyan.

Krishna had thus recommended Sanyasa (renunciation) of actions and again praised Yoga, which put Arjuna in confusion and desired to know as to which was better of the two. Krishna told that Sanyasa and Karma Yoga both affected certain well-being but of the two, Karma Yoga was superior. A person, who neither hated nor desired anything, was free from pairs of opposites, such a person is verily and easily released from the bondage. One without knowledge only spoke of distinctness of Sankhya and Yoga but one well established in even one of them obtained the fruit of both. The place attained by Sankhya is reached by Yogis. Therefore, the wise was he who saw that Sankhya and Yoga were one. Here Krishna did not recommend to Arjuna Sanyasa or Karma Yoga, one in preference to the other, while giving his opinion that Karma Yoga excelled Karma Sanyasa and not Sanyasa. This was not to dissuade Arjuna from Sanyasa or Yoga Karma as following any of the two his well-being was assured but between Karma Yoga and Karma Sanyasa, the former excelled the latter, which would imply that he wanted Arjuna to adopt the former in preference to the latter. But Sanyasa without Yoga was difficult to be attained, only a Yogi, harmonised Muni attained to Brahma. For Arjuna, Krishna recommended Yoga which required that he should not abstain and explained to him the attitude he should adopt. One harmonised in Yoga speedily attained to Brahma, which in other words meant that he attained his highest well-being and this is what Arjuna wanted to be clarified. Krishna's mention of Muni, harmonised in Yoga was with the purpose to convey that such person rested in Sattava beyond the influence of the agitating and coursing Rajas, which constituted speech, and beyond the objective Tamas, which the speech impuned itself. He is not the speech any more than are the actions which the Prakriti, left to itself, generated. Once Yoga is harmonised, the perfectly pure self, the victorious self, one who has conquered the senses, himself the self of all beings even though acting, he is not polluted. He feels he had been doing nothing, but his seeing, hearing, touching, smelling, eating, going about, sleeping, breathing, speaking, exerting, grasping, opening and closing the eyes even thinking that the senses had been moving among the sense objects, who foregoing attachment, performed actions without any sins and dedicated them to Brahma.

Thus abandoning any attachment, the Yogis performed actions by body, Manas and Budhi, all through the senses only. Thus harmonised, abandoning the fruit of action, he attains everlasting peace and the non- harmonised by reason of desire (Kama) attached to fruits reverts back to the universe. Thus Arjuna was told about the Sanyasa, which was compatible with actions having been renounced – actions which the Yoga did not disallow, nor he resorted to abstention for which there was no justification. Here he is told that Sanyasa did not mean that there shall be no Yoga. On the contrary it is said that action with Yoga is established which meant safety and well-being and that without Yoga meant danger, sin and bondage. So Sanyasa and Yoga – both meant well-being and Sanyasa was essentially one with it. Yoga did not, therefore, mean that there should be no action nor did Sanyasa mean that one should avoid or prevent it. Wherever there was Prakriti, there would be action and neither a Yogi nor a Sanyasi should concern himself with prakriti or what pertained to it and, therefore, with action too which it generated. In view of this the Prakriti with its Rajas Guna individualised every being, not excepting even a Yogi or a Sanyasi, actions were inevitable and they appeared in a Yogi as much as in a non-yogi. Then what is to be avoided and guarded against is not so much action as attachment to it or its fruits. A Yogi foregoes all attachment for the fruit of actions and a non-Yogi by virtue of desires (Kama) which burned in him was attached to fruits. Without depending on the fruits of action, if one performs action that ought to be done, he is Sanyasi and a Yogi and not the fireless (without fire of you) and the non-acting. One might be a Sanyasi or a Yogi, he has to perform action or rather allow actions which are ordained and which his Prakriti would determine, only such a person shall seek any shelter in or feel concerned for, what they affect and what their fruits would be. So engaged in action which he ought to allow, one is as much a Sanyasi as he is a Yogi and one striving to put out the fire of Gyan or thus being fireless, he by perpetuating the mould which served only to smother and extinguish the fire would be neither a Sanyasi nor a yogi. Either he be, therefore, a Sanyasi or a Yogi in neither case he could justify abstention. Even for a muni wishing to rise to Yoga, karma (action) is said to be his means and for one established in Yoga, Sham (Tranquillity) is said to be the means. When neither in sense objects nor in actions one felt attached, then with all Sankalpas renounced 'Yoga-arudha' (established in Yoga) he is called. Therefore, let one by the self raise up the self, not destroy the self for verily the self is the self's friend and the self itself is the self's enemy. It is by self only that the self is conquered. In the enmity of even the non-self it is the self that behaves like the enemy. The supreme self is evenly balanced in cold and heat, pleasure and pain and honour and insult. The Gyan-Vigyan satiated self, the one with the senses well-subdued and harmonised, which is styled by the Yogi seeing sameness in a lump of clay and stone and gold. One in Budhi same in lovers, friends, foes and in those who are indifferent, in neutrals, haters and relatives and also in the righteous and the unrighteous, is esteemed. The Yogi should constantly centralise the self, resting in solitude, alone, himself with Chitta controlled, free from all expectations and appropriating nothing. He should establish his seat in a pure site, neither too high nor too low, spread over by Kusha grass, or the skin of an antelope, and a cloth one over the other. Then making his Manas one-pointed, with the functioning of his Chitta and senses controlled, taking his seat, he should engage in Yoga for self-purification keeping his body, back and neck balanced and immovably steady, himself firm, gazing fixedly at his own tip of the nose and not looking in any direction, the self fearless, established in vow of a Brahamchari, having well controlled mind, with Chitta fixed on God, harmonised he should rest interest in God. Centralising thus constantly the self, a Yogi with Manas well-controlled attained to the Supreme peace of Nirvana abiding in God. Pain destroying Yoga is attained by one, harmonised in eating and going about, and with harmonised movements in actions, one harmonised in sleep and waking. If everything is empty of inherent, independent existence, then why are we sometimes happy and other times depressed and miserable and why good and bad things happen to people? For this one explanation is that ignorance of the empty nature of things still pervades our minds and until we free our minds from ignorance we will continue to have problems and another explanation is that although everything is empty on the ultimate level of reality on the relative or conventional level the experiences we have are subject to law of cause and effect or Karma. Karma means "action" and it refers to the process whereby the actions we do are the causes of effects or results that we will experience in the future. Therefore, the law of karma is also known as the law of cause and effect. People, sometimes wonder if the law of karma applies only to those who believe in it and not to those who do not know about or believe in it. If that were the case, it would be better to not to know about karma. In reality, karma is a universal law that applies to all beings, whether they know about and believe in it or not. It is similar to gravity – all beings are subject to gravity, whether they are aware of it or not. Another common question is whether karma means that we have no free will. For those who are unaware of karma, there is little or no free will because they do not know the causes of good and bad experiences. Those who know about karma are free to act in ways that will bring the happiness they wish for, and avoid the problems they do not want. So karma means that we are the creators and we are responsible for our experiences, rather than an external creator or other people and circumstances. Some people have no trouble accepting karma they may even have had an intuitive understanding of it their whole life. Others are sceptical and ask for proof. But it is difficult to come up with concrete proof because karma is in the mind and the mind is non-material. But we can see the working of the karma in our own life.

When we are in bad state of mind – dissatisfied with ourselves and our life, or angry at the world – then everything will go wrong and we will attract problems but when we are in good state of mind and treat people with respect and consideration, we are much more likely to have good experiences. So our own experiences are proof that our attitude and behaviour affects what happens to us in our daily life. The purpose of meditating on karma is two-fold: to develop the awareness that we are responsible – we are the creators of our own experiences – and to learn which actions bring suffering so we can avoid those, and which actions lead to happiness, we can engage in them. We should generate a positive motivation for doing the meditation, such as wanting to have a better understanding of karma so that we can avoid doing actions that bring problems to ourselves and others and can be more beneficial, both to ourselves and others. This means that there is a definite co-relation between the actions we do and the experiences we have in that negative actions bring problems, not happiness, and positive actions bring happiness, not suffering. It can never be otherwise. It is similar to what happens in nature – if we plant pumpkin seeds we get pumpkin, not chilli and if we plant chilli, we get chilli not pumpkin. This also means that if we do a negative action, even a minor one, and do not apply any opponent force such as purification practice, the Kama increases continuously and will bring many unpleasant results and on the positive side, one small positive action, if not opposed to by a negative one, will bring many positive results. Further, if we do not do negative actions we will not have bad experiences in future. This principle explains why some are killed or injured in a car accident while others walk away even without a scratch, or why some fail in starting a business even though they have an M.B.A. while others are successful though they have never been to a business school. On the other hand if we do not do any positive actions, we will not experience any good results in the future. Wishing to be happy and successful but not creating the right causes would be like wishing for flowers or vegetables to grow in our garden but not doing the work of planting the seeds, watering the small shoots, removing the weeds and so on. This principle can also be understood in terms of our present experiences. Any time, if we experience a problem or any unhappy state of mind, this is necessarily due to negative karma we created in the past. Now when we do an action – physical, verbal or mental – an imprint, like a seed, is planted in our mind and unless we do something to counteract that karmic seed, it will remain in the mind, even for many life-times, until we encounter the right causes and conditions for it to ripen in the form of experiences, good or bad. How can the karmic seeds be counteracted, for this we can clear away negative karma by doing a purification practice using the four opponent powers like feeling regret, relying on helpful objects, and refuge in Dharma and doing actions to balance things out as also to resolve not to do such actions again? When first contemplating karma, we may feel a sense of heaviness and even fear, similar to the way we would feel if our doctor told us we have a serious illness. But as there are methods to deal with illness – medicines, treatment, dieting and lifestyle changing, and working on our mind to learn to accept it – there are methods for working on karma but we have to remember that it is not like fate, fixed and unchangeable, so it can be changed and there is no negative that cannot be purified. After meditating on karma we will probably feel uncomfortable about the negative actions we have done and the consequences we are likely to face in the future. But there is a solution to this – the practice of purification. Negative karma is not something fixed, permanent and irreparable. The imprints left on our mind from our negative actions can be purified so that we do not have to experience the suffering results that would otherwise come and so we can clear this negative energy out of the way of our spiritual development. That is a reason for purification. There is no negative that cannot be purified. The purification process basically is a psychological one. The practice of purification involves contemplating the four opponent powers – regret, reliance, remedy and resolve. Regret involves recognising that certain actions we have done are negative because they harmed others or ourselves because they will bring more problems later on and also because we were acting on an ego-centred, deluded way. Regret is not the same as guilt. Guilt comes from non-understanding the true nature of things and believing that we have a real, permanent self or "I". We focus on things we have done wrong. Regret on the other hand is intelligent and constructive. It is based on the understanding of karma that negative actions such as killing or hurting others cause suffering to them as well as to ourselves, both now and in future. Regret is linked to the way we would feel if we found out that something we had swallowed was poisonous. We regret our mistakes and do whatever we can to clear up the karma. Reliance power is like when we fall down on the ground, we rely on the ground to get up again. Similarly when we do something negative, it is either in relation to pure beings such as a saint or our spiritual leader or in relation to ordinary satient being, so in order to purify our negative karma, we need to recall or rely on the spiritual leader or rely on other beings by developing compassion or love. The power of remedy means doing something positive in order to counteract the negative energy we have created. In general, any positive action can be used to purify our negative karma. The next step i.e. the power of resolve is making the determination not to repeat the same negative actions again. The resolve in general is to make the effort to avoid the old habits. This determination not to do the negative actions again is what gives us strength to turn ourselves around for which we have to have confidence in our ability to change. The question of suffering has always perplexed all beings even the philosophers. Why is there so much fighting, starvation, sickness, inequality and injustice, the main causes of suffering? The first cause is that the suffering does exist. It refers to any experience that is unpleasant and unsatisfactory. Secondly suffering always has a cause and the principle cause of suffering is Kama and delusions i.e. anger, attachment and ignorance. Thirdly, there is an end to suffering as we all have a potential to reach a state of perfect peace, clarity, compassion, in which we no longer experience the results of past negative acts or create the causes for further suffering. Fourth, there is a means to end suffering. The way to end suffering is to gradually abandon its causes – anger, selfishness, attachment and other negative states of mind and actions motivated by these – and cultivate the causes of happiness – patience, love, non-attachment and generosity and other positive states of mind. Successful meditation on suffering brings us to more realistic view of life, and by understanding that the causes of suffering lie in our own attitudes and actions, we will gradually come to see that unravelling the complexities of our mind and thus developing control over our thoughts and actions is both desirable and possible.

# Chapter X

## Sufferings by Human Beings

There are three aspects of suffering to contemplate:

1. <u>Suffering of suffering</u>: this includes all obvious forms of suffering, physical and mental such as suffering arising from war, terrorism, natural disasters, famine, injustice, racism, illness etc. and also includes all the normal everyday problems our body experiences as pains, heat, cold, hunger, thirst etc. For this we have to contemplate the fact that it is the nature of the body to change, meet with pain and eventually die. Therefore, it is unrealistic and unwise to be attached to it and cling to it as "me".

2. <u>Suffering of change</u>: This more stable level of suffering refers to the experience we normally think of as pleasure or happiness. They become suffering because they do not last. Every nice experience comes to an end without fully satisfying us.

3. <u>All pervading suffering</u>: This is even more subtle than the suffering of change. It refers to our very existence as

ordinary, un-enlightened beings with our mind caught up inextricably in delusions and kama.

Although the nature of our mind is clear and has the potential to experience the pure, enduring peace and bliss of enlightenment, we are unable to keep it free of disturbed, unhappy thoughts and feelings even for an hour. Lacking a direct, intuitive insight in to our true nature of things, we think, speak and act under the control of delusions, our habitual negative tendencies. We are thus in a bind and on the one hand we experience in every moment the effects of previous karma and delusion and on the other we create every moment the causes for further effects. In either case we should not panic and consider the situation not hopeless as there is a way out of this cycle. Just as there is a cause of suffering – our false view of the way things exists – there is necessarily a cause of the end of this suffering, an antidote. In the meantime we can use our life and energy in positive ways like helping others with love and generosity and increasing the positive thoughts and attitudes in our mind. Further, the sufferings and problems are not necessarily bad, it depends on our attitude. If we feel averse to them as completely useless and unwanted, then we will suffer more. But if we have a more realistic view, seeing them as a natural part of life, then we can accept them calmly. In addition by learning to use them in our path of spiritual growth, we can even feel glad when they occur.

The goal of meditation is to reach the state of perfect wholeness enlightenment in order to alleviate the suffering of others, bring them happiness and finally lead them to their own enlightenment. We can start to cultivate the mind of enlightenment now in our day-to-day lives by being kind and open to people we meet. But we meet people, interact with them briefly in positive or negative ways and then separate. Nothing lasts and nothing is stable. The more we cling to this unreal "I" and try to fulfil its demands, the deeper we bury ourselves in problems and confusion. Our classification of people into 'friends', 'enemies' and 'strangers' is probably the best example of this. We assume that a person we like has inherently good qualities and the person we dislike is inherently bad. We behave as though these qualities are permanent and unchanging; as though we will always be close to the persons we have labelled 'friend' and never close to the person we dislike and it is hard to imagine that an uninteresting person in the street could ever become a friend. But these assumptions are mistaken as our own experiences tell us. Relationship can and do change, people change, our thoughts change, feelings change and situations change.

We now come to meditation on love. Love also called "Love kindness" wants others to be happy. It is a natural quality of mind, but until we develop through meditation and other practices it remains limited, reserved for a few selected individuals – usually those we are attached and genuine love is universal in scope, extending to every one without exception. Although we might agree with this idea in principle, we probably find it difficult to actualise. We should begin with mindfulness, observing our reactions to the people we encounter, looking out for feelings of attraction, aversion and indifference. As long as we continue to discriminate between those we like, those we dislike and those we do not care about, we can never even take the first step. Some meditations such as that on the breath and emptiness involve meditating on an object. Other meditations such as on love and compassion involve transferring the mind into the object we are meditating upon. So ideally when we do the meditation, our mind truely experiences love. Then we should meditate on love for others, starting with one family and close friends sitting near us and then think of some people we are not close to like neighbours, our colleagues in office, school etc. and then to turn our attention to the people in front of us and those we have difficulty with, contemplating that they also need and deserve our love. In this way we would think that we definitely have the potential to love everyone, even those who annoy or hurt us and those we do not know even. As mindfulness develops we become increasingly sensitive to our thoughts and feelings, including negative states of mind such as anger, irritation, pride, depression, desire and so forth. Why are these considered "negative" because they are delusions – distorted conceptions that paint a false picture of reality – and because they lead to unhappiness, confusion and problems. The root cause of the negative emotions is the false notion of inherent graspable, solid existence that we impute on to every-thing. This misconception gives rise to attachment to whatever appears pleasant, aversion or anger towards whatever is unpleasant and painful and an uneasing ignorance about everything else.

However, like our experiences, negative emotions are impermanent, neither fixed nor concrete, they are simply mental energy like love and joy whose nature is clear and non-material. For this a more skilful approach is to honestly acknowledge the presence of emotion, but step back and observe it in a detached way within the calm spaciousness of meditation. Then an important first step in working with emotions is recognising and identifying them. The second step is having a healthy balanced attitude towards the negative emotions. The next step is to work on the delusion in meditation, using one or more antidotes explained above. If a number of different emotions disturb then we have to eliminate them one-by-one. These methods provide new ways of looking at these emotions and are not magical solutions to what are after all our difficulties. Attachment is to want something and not want to be separated from it and it is also known as desire. Attachment is difficult to detect and more difficult to find fault with. We think it is the road to happiness and satisfaction but fulfilment of desire is an allusion as desire leads to more desire, not satisfaction.

We see how attachment to alcohol, drugs or money leads to problems rather than happiness but we may wonder what is wrong in attachment with people. Would not the life be empty and meaningless without family and friends? But when a relationship involves attachment, problems invariably arise. We become dependent on good feelings and comfort of relationship and then suffer when it changes. Overcoming attachment does not mean becoming cold and indifferent. On the contrary, detachment means learning to have relaxed control over our mind through understanding the real causes of happiness and fulfilment and this enables us to enjoy life more and suffer less. For dealing with attachment we have to first contemplate the faults of attachment. Think of the suffering we experience when we separate from an object of attachment. We all know the pain of relationships that did not work and the grief over a loved one's death. If we recall that all things are impermanent and by nature they change from moment to moment and will inevitably perish, the object of attachment will not be attractive and pleasing. We have to remember that death is inevitable and that it could come any time separating us from our nearest. Therefore, the best remedy to attachment and all other delusions is to think of emptiness, investigate the "I" that experiences attachment and try to locate this seemingly reality, solid in our mind and body. If we feel strongly attached to an attractive body (including our own) we should at first analyse just what it is that we find attractive. Similarly, a remedy for attachment to food is to contemplate the suffering experienced by all the beings involved in its preparation. Animals are killed; innumerable small insects are killed; insects are killed in cultivation and spraying of grains, fruits, vegetables that we eat. We should try to eat mindfully with appreciation for all beings' kindness and sacrifice.

# Chapter XI

## Anger, Depression and Fear

As opposed to attachment – wanting not to be separated from something or someone – anger is the attitude of wanting to be separated, of wanting to harm. Most of our anger is directed towards other people but we can also be angry at ourselves or an intimate object. Anger is the very opposite of patience, tolerance, compassion and love. Anger distorts our view of things. So after examining it we should apply an antidote such as the one of the methods below:

1. Contemplate the faults or disadvantages of anger so that we become convinced that it is harmful rather than helpful and, therefore, not something we want to indulge in.

2. Remember karma, cause and effect. If someone harms us in some way by being abusive or unfriendly, cheating or stealing from us or wrecking our belongings and it seems we have done nothing to deserve it, check again.

3. Another method for dealing with the people who hurt or annoy us is to put ourselves in their place and try to see the situation from their point of view.

4. Should not see faults in others if we did have those faults in ourselves.

5. Anger is more likely to arise in our mind when we are unhappy or dissatisfied. We should in such a case sit down and check what is going on in the deeper level of our minds.

6. When anger arises, we should turn our attention within and investigate the "I" that is angry. Analyse when and how it existed and then use antidotes.

7. Difficult situations are unusually the most productive in terms of spiritual growth. Thus someone who arouses anger is giving a chance to learn that we still have work to do.

8. Having gained some control over our anger through one of these methods, we might like to work on developing love. We can do these by practising the meditation on love, visualising in front of us the person who made us angry and making a special effort to actually reverse our feeling for them.

9. Contemplate the points of death meditation. Death could happen any time so realise that it is senseless to cling to differences with people.

All the methods explained above involve meditating to try to deal with anger on our own, it is also possible to resolve a conflict by communicating with the other persons, but we have to consider whether or not the other person would be open to such communication and if it would bring positive results. If we start discussion with the desire to hurt or with expectations and demands the communication will not work. Of course sometimes anger is very strong and the lasting thing we feel like doing is sitting down to meditate.

**Depression:** There are following ways to eliminate depression:

1. Take a step back from our thoughts and feelings and check what they are saying. Depression often involves repetitive, self-critical thoughts such as "I am worthless", "Nobody cares for me," "I never do anything right". If we are honest to ourselves, we will recognise that these thoughts are mistaken or exaggerated, focussing on the negative and ignoring the positive. Do the meditation on appreciating our human life and then the positive energy still remaining in us will prevail.

2. Meditate on the clarity of our mind, our happiness, our worry, frustration as well as our good feelings are all just mental energy – clear, no physical and otherwise. Do not, therefore, involve in such thoughts taking that all experiences are impermanent.

3. Investigate the "I", our sense of self that identifies strongly with unhappy thoughts and feelings. Try to find if this depressed "I" is something permanent, solid, unchanging.

4. Meditate on love or compassion, and turning outwards towards others and contemplating their needs but it should not be suffering to us.

5. Do one of the visualisation meditations viz. the body of light or purification meditation. These can be quick ways to cut through our depression.

6. A very effective remedy for depression is to get out and help others. Do some voluntary service; doing physical excursion also has the same effect.

**Fear:** It is a common cause of unhappiness and stress. Fear is not necessarily negative; it depends on what we are afraid of and how we handle our fears. The root cause of fear and anxiety is our misconception of our "I" and all other things seeing them as solid, real and permanent. The following methods can get relief from fear:

1. Look at the fear. Sit down and make mind calm with some breathing meditation. Then allow the fear to come into the clear spaciousness of the mind. Do not let get caught up in it but stand back and examine it and then ask ourselves if it was reasonable for me to have fear.

2. If we are afraid of change, loss or death, we can meditate the impermanence and death familiarising ourselves with the reality of life.

3. Contemplate how it is in the nature of unenlightened existence to encounter problems and painful and undesirable experiences.

4. The root of fear is our mistaken conception of the way we and everyone and everything exists. It is useful to meditate on emptiness. When we have fear, we should go within and examine the "I" that is frightened.

5. Some people find it helpful to bring to mind an object of refuge when they feel frightened. This could be God or other enlightened being. Even if nothing amazing happens outside of us, taking refuge and praying helps us to feel more calm and courageous inside and better able to handle the difficult situations we are in.

**Devotion:** The idea of devotion makes some people uneasy because they equate it with blind faith and mindless submissiveness. But proper devotion is not like that. It is in fact a very positive attitude to be devoted to one's family, friend or work to have love, care and responsibility. In this sense it means going beyond our usual narrow self-centred thoughts and concerns and dedicating our energy to others. In religious or spiritual sense, devotion involves faith, which is a mental state and is explained as clarity, conviction and aspiration with regard to someone or something that exists and has excellent qualities and abilities. There are three kinds of faiths – one is recognising and appreciating the good qualities of a person or object, another is aspiring to emulate those qualities and the third is conviction based on having studied and contemplated the teaching given by someone. Ofcourse, if our faith and devotion are not well-founded or their object is unreliable we will only be disappointed and feel doubt and resentment. But if it is based on clear and correct understanding and its object is one that will not let us down, the experience will be rich and productive. Refuge is a fundamental step on the spiritual path and devotion is an essential component of it. It should not be an ignorant, emotional attitude but one that is sound and intelligent, based on clear understanding of what Dharma really is and what it can do for us. We do need help to travel the path to inner awakening but we need to check carefully the qualifications of the teachers we meet and the effectiveness of their methods not just follow the advice of anyone with a nice vibration or a charismatic personality.

**Prayer:** The success of any project – climbing a mountain, writing a book or baking a cake – hinges on the care we take in the preparatory work. The same is true of meditation. A successful meditation session depends primarily on our state of mind and the appropriate inner state can be induced through reciting certain prayers, verbally or mentally, with understanding and sincerity. Prayer is not the mechanical repetition of words but is opening of the heart to communicate with our true nature. The words serve as a reminder of what we are trying to achieve, and actually help create the cause for whatever we are praying for to occur in the future. The prayer expresses the most positive, beneficial intention we could have for engaging in study to meditate on the path to enlightenment. A part of the prayer is taking refuge in Him. The second part is the generation of Bodhichitta, the mind set on enlightenment. Bodhichitta founded in pure love and compassion for every loving being is the dedicated determination to become devotee solely to help others achieve enlightenment too. The thoughts expressed in the prayer are called immeasurable, because they extend to all beings throughout the infinite universe. The first is the immeasurable love, the wish for all beings to be free from sufferings; the second is immeasurable compassion, the wish for all beings to be happy; the third is immeasurable joy, the wish for all beings to experience the ultimate happiness that lasts forever; the fourth is immeasurable equanimity, the wish for all beings to be free of the attachment and aversion that cause us to distinguish between friend, enemy and stranger.

Why, when we sit down to meditate does our mind wander helplessly here and there? Why it is so difficult to control the mind and attain realisation? Perhaps we imagine that things were easier before we started meditation. Transforming the mind is not easy, so it is not surprising that we experience obstacles and problems. It is not that we lack wisdom or the ability to meditate properly, to penetrate deep into the mind; rather we are distracted because of the negative energy of our delusions; our distorted conceptions and emotions, which have been accumulating since beginningless time. When we sit down to meditate, this energy manifests physically our discomfort or restlessness and mutually as sleepiness, agitation, tension or doubt. Our weak wisdom frame exists but it is no match for this dark storm of negative energy. One of the characteristics of karma is that it increases with time, in the same way that one fruit seed results in many fruits. It is obvious, then, that to prevent the results of negative actions, increasing it is necessary to purify our mind of imprints left by negative actions of body, speech and mind.

**Purification of body:** Our delusions and negativities in general, and particularly those of the body take the form of black ink and sicknesses and afflictions caused by spirits take the form of scorpions, snakes, frogs and crabs. Flushed out by the light and nectar, they all leave 0ur body through the lower openings, like filthy water flowing from a drain pipe. We are now completely emptied of those problems, they no longer exists anywhere.

**Purification of speech:** Our delusions and the imprints of negativities of speech take the form of liquid tar. The light and nectar fill our body as water fills a dirty glass and the negativities, like the dirt in the glass, rise to the top and flow out through the upper openings of the body. We are now completely emptied of those problems, they no longer exist anywhere.

**Purification of mind:** Our delusions and imprints of mental negativities appear as darkness at our heart. When struck by the forceful stream of light and nectar, the darkness instantly disappears and we are completely emptied of these problems. They no longer exist anywhere.

# Chapter XII

# Dharma

The exponents of Dharamshastras distinguish three principle sources of Dharma – The Vedas, Smiritis and Sadachar or Sishtachar. The conduct of people who are virtuous (Sat) and learned (Sista) while the Dharamshastras uphold this three-fold model, the Manusmriti and Yajnawalka Smriti adds a fourth source, that which satisfies the self (Atmatushti, Priyamatwak). The Veda, Smriti, Sadachar and that which is pleasing to us – they declare this explicitly to be the four-fold means of defining Dharma. The supreme source of Dharma is Shruti (Vedas). Manusmriti declares that any tradition or philosophy that is not based on Vedas is worthless and untrue and produces no reward after death.

While traditions that are not based on Vedas arise and pass away, the Vedas are eternal, beyond human power and beyond measure. Vedas are thus represented as the source of Dharma, both in its ontological function as the cosmic aduing principle and in its normative function as the social adu. Vedas are considered also the ultimate source of all the specific rules of Dharma delineated in the

Dharamshastras and Dharamsutras. Varanashrama system constitutes the paradigmatic expression of the cosmic adu on the human plane of existence. In this model of social order, at the beginning of each cycle of creation, the principle of Dharma in accordance with the eternal Vedas, establishes the separation of functions among the various classes of gods, plants, animals and other beings in the divine and natural orders and also establishes the separate functions among the various classes of human beings that constitute the social order.

Bhagwat Gita provides a meditating position between the perspective of Dharamshastras, which govern precedence to Dharma and the perspective of renunciation tradition which give priority to Moksha. Lord Krishna exhorts Arjuna to emulate the divine example and prepare his Dharma for the welfare of the world while remaining established in the non-active self (Atman) which exists in a perpetual state of non-attachment from the ever active relative field. It is ignorance of the true nature of self as separate from the field of activity that gives rise to bondage. Gita maintains that liberation from this state of bondage cannot be gained by simply renouncing the world and attempting to abandon all actions for not by abstaining from actions does a man attain non-action and not by mere renunciation does he achieve perfection. The key to Moksha lies in developing a state of consciousness in which the sage realises the true nature of the self as separate from the field of activity and thus ceases to claim authorship for actions. The sage who becomes established in this inner state of non-attachment, in which the fruits of actions are spontaneously relinquished, is the true renunciation – not the person who simply adopts the life-style of an ascetic and attempts to abandon the world of actions. He, who performs action, that is his duty, without depending on the fruit of action, is Sanyasin and a Yogin, not he who is without fire and also abstains from religious rites. As a means of gaining direct experience of self, Gita advocates the practice of meditation and suggests that such meditation practices are not to be restricted to Gyan Yoga, leading a renuncient way of life but are also to be undertaken by the Karam Yogins actively involved in the world. Having become established in the self, the silent witness of the realm of action, the Yogin should engage in action and perform his Dharma free from attachment, in a state of equanimity. This state of non-attachment culminates in the surrender of all actions and their fruits to the supreme source the Lord of Creation itself. Gyan Yoga, the Yoga of knowledge; Karamyoga, the Yoga of action and Dhyanyoga, the Yoga of meditation, finds their fulfilment in Bhakti Yoga the Yoga of devotion to the Lord.

Dharma is a way of life, practising which one attains the supreme aim of salvation. Practice and process to follow may be different in different Dharmas but the destination of all is to attain salvation. The correct practice of Dharma is derived from a teacher, who received it from another teacher and it has come down in a long lineage this way. Actually it is the truth and does not reside in any particular person and if we respect the person or a teacher and only act out of deference to him, this is not Dharma. This we shall be doing just fulfilling our duties because we see the teacher around and when he has gone away, slacken. The teaching of Dharma enables humans to enter the stream and see themselves, when we see ourselves, we see Dharma and seeing Dharma we see the almighty and thus we have entered the stream. In teaching Dharma, things have to be repeated over and over again for people to gain real understanding. It is what has to be done in order to get the important points across. When it really touches the mind, one desists from harming oneself and others and gives up the three poisons of desire, anger and delusion. But some will hear and call it wrong because it does not agree with their opinions and habits. Actually the things that agree with the sentient beings' mind are not always good. Good speech is always straight, direct and upright, which has the purpose of reducing the emotional afflictions and getting free of delusions. Such words do not merely try to follow peoples' personal preferences and some would even say that if it disagreed with them it was a good speech.

For teaching Dharma, a language is used which is tool to help us understand. Even though we have not yet attained realisation, we should put language to work and contemplate it. For instance, if we hear laziness and negligence are not good, we apply our minds and when laziness arises it is found nowhere but in the mind only. In

Dharma we reduce and transfer the laziness to our understanding. We have to listen to Dharma for the purpose of knowing how to practice Dharma. For this we see Dharma and enter Dharma which shows all things as they really are. Living beings ate material objects as well as the inner phenomena of feeling and thinking. All this is Dharma. In this there are two categories – objects that can be seen by the eyes or known by the other senses and mind, which cannot be seen that way. They are just our body and mind and nothing away from us but Dharma arises independent of our wishes from causes and conditions which change in the middle and then end, break up and disappear. The Dharma has power above all this, it cannot be greater or lesser and so have their own mode of existence according to its causes. Take the body for instance it is born of causes and conditions. When we become older our bodies change according to their nature. In the beginning it is born according to causes it develops by conditions and in the end it will break up not depending on any one's wishes or orders but according to the law of nature. They do not need to ask permission or agreement of any of us to help them grow, age, wither and die. This all happens itself and we do not have authority over it and we have to accept that it is all natural. If our awareness of this truth is not clear and we are instead deluded about nature, it is called the Dharma of delusion.

Then we see the things as self, as ours and in terms of self and others. This is ignorance and when there is ignorance, mental formation arises. We struggle with things. We want to control to get one or avoid the other and thus fall prey to our likes and dislikes. But these are not really Dharma. Whatever we may believe has its existence according to nature and merely that. But if we have awareness that knows according to Dharma, we know it is nature and merely that. The body experiences birth, aging and death. There is nothing stable in it and if we know Dharma then we realise it is birth and there is nothing to change. Destroy ourselves of the truth and we come to this point there is nothing more to say. Thus seeing natural conditions arising and changing is called studying Dharma and having learnt it we should train our minds without having cravings for worldly belongings to be Dharma only. When we start to identify with our bodies and minds and think of this life as ours, then we are like a traveller in this universe, who does not like to learn it but leave he must is knowing Dharma. All Dharmas arise from causes and conditions. When the causes and conditions exist, the result occurs accordingly. It is just the law of nature and when it breaks up that is also nature. This law is called Dharma.

Then there is the Dharma of practising a code of conduct, people living together with restraint and consideration. This too is Dharma or the way of virtuous behaviour. It is Dharma that the populace at large needs to practise for happiness but this happiness is first attained as the beginning of suffering but still we make this happiness and keeping it leads to suffering but when we listen to Dharma, we do not think that is all there is to do. Our aim is to know Dharma and when we see Dharma, the sufferings end. Outside of the Dharma, there is nothing that can bring us to live in harmony together and to go beyond suffering and unsatisfactory experience and to realise happiness and tranquillity. Dharma is far superior to anything we can find at home. The things at home generally bring only trouble and do not cause peace. These are only things for worry, concern and struggle rather than the things that stale us. If we practise Dharma like this we would come to know that Dharma really does have value but it is necessary to understand, to contemplate and to practice it. Thus if we think the things are real then there would be suffering and fear. All this is just the carrying on of people as to what is actually happening, there is nothing and there is nothing to laugh or cry over, nothing worthy of love or hate in itself.

It is only the mind being tricked. Therefore, what is needed is to correct the mind without which we believe that we exist as self-entities and that the things belonged to us. This in fact is just being deluded. Dharma teaches us to come out of it by bridling our mind, although a difficult task. Therefore, we should not take anything – the body in good or bad health, the mind in elation or depression – as being too real as we only destroy ourselves by doing that. It is here that within us the things are happening, which result being born from causes, there is really nothing. It is our grasping that makes the things appearing like that. Not seeing Dharma we are always thinking them as real although they are not. We, therefore, should understand that all the things we practice are for leading the mind to see Dharma and to be Dharma. If we see Dharma then although we have the habit of anger and have desire, even if they return they will come with decreasing energy if we get absorbed in Dharma, even if we do not change or improve Dharma. So Dharma is truth and if we reach the truth, there would be no big or small, no happiness or suffering but only peace.

If there is ever thinking of mind it would be all peace. It is like having one chair in a house, you sit there and when others come they have nowhere to sit. Mind is like this. The mental afflictions may come but because Dharma is in the mind, they have nowhere to sit down and so they will have to go their way. The path and defilement fight each other in this way. If the path is brought to fullness, then when things happen in the mind we meet the Dharma. This takes the person with energy and one who is not energetic will retreat at this point. Similarly if there is no one at home, unwanted guests can come and make them comfortable. They sit down, eat and make mess. This certainly one does not want and, therefore, makes his own home inhabited only by Dharma. This is Dharma and realising fruition, knowing Dharma and practising it is necessary and this is the way in which Dharma bears fruits.

# Chapter XIII

## Dharma in Practice

We practise Dharma because we see the value of noble treasure, the wealth that is within. We have attachment to material wealth but now we try to exchange it for inner wealth. This kind of wealth shall be free from the dangers of the elements, such as flood, fire or that of thieves. It is something that cannot be found by them and as such, no external threats can touch this happiness of mind. Making offerings is one source of such happiness, because then we overcome the tendencies towards greed and miserliness. Whatever Dharma practice we are doing viz. giving and keeping moral precepts or meditating on loving – kindness towards all beings - they all come to a single point that is the pursuit of peace. Birth, youth, aging, poverty, riches and so forth are all sufferings if we do not know them. We should, therefore, know dukha and other noble truths, the cause, the cessation and the holy path and if we do know, there is nothing to suffer over. Suffering, therefore, is a fixed part of the mind that it has been there forever but suffering is not intrinsic to the mind, it arises any moment. One has aversion in the mind and the suffering starts.

But the practising of Dharma is the only cure for such sufferings. In Dharma, we are taught to begin with right understanding, then there are right thoughts, right actions, right speech, right livelihood, right effort, right mindfulness and right meditation. We say them right only but they are really factors of the one path upon which each individual must travel. When understanding is correct, thinking will be correct and so will speech and all other factors and when the mind is established in what is correct, the entire progression of the path must be correct. Nothing will be wrong and walking the path will lead to peace. But we always see in terms of my leg, my hand, my friend, my house etc. Thus we are self only. But according to Dharma, it is not seeing self. Understanding that these are not self is seeing self. We see it but do not carry it. All things are subject to change and being attached to them can only produce experience that is unsatisfactory and make us sometimes happy and sometimes upset. If there is right view then feeling is merely feeling. Pleasure is merely pleasure. Pain is merely pain. There is no owner either of pain or pleasure. When we come to know about these phenomena, and do not get so involved with them, the mind becomes peaceful because we are no longer trying to own anything.

But still we can enjoy our lives and make use of the things in the world. We use them but it is in order to gain the realisation that they are not ours. We use them but without having to suffer over them. If we cannot be above all these things, we are under them carrying them with the attachment that says "This is mine". This wrong view can only lead to suffering because things will never work out as we desire. But people want happiness, riches and so forth. They are attached to merit only wanting tangible benefits but not making real spiritual progress. In arithmetic there are adding, subtracting, multiplying and dividing but we only want adding and multiplying. Actually we can say that these are ourselves and things are ours but that is only a conventional reality. It is not on the even level of liberation. We need to learn about the way we use conventions in all aspects of our lives, for example our names. When we were born we did not bring names with us and after we came in this universe, we were given names. There was not an old name to be replaced but it was empty there. Actually there was no one there just natural conditions but we having given names are known by those names only disregarding the natural conditions. Having been born, things pass away. Having passed away things are born again. So birth and passing away all conditions are like that only. It is, therefore, better we do work for the sake of doing it, while realising that there is no self involved and nothing belonged to us and training our mind to let go. This is the right view or right understanding. Saying that this world is empty might give us the idea that there is nothing in the world but when we look at a bowl or a spittoon, these things do exist. It is not that they do not exist but they exist in the sphere of emptiness. We can call a spittoon as a convention that we create through one designation or we can call it a pot. Actually it is empty of these names from its own side but we view it in a certain way and then have attachment to seeing it as such.

Having discussed all this we again come to Dharma. Dharma means all things, the forms that the eyes see, sounds heard by ear, these are all Dharmas because Dharma means conditions that are maintained in existence. Having come in to being, they pass away and we do not need to expect too much from them, because that is the way they are. We should rather internalise this truth and see it in our minds and bodies, it is not something far away. The components of body are not stable or permanent and have no reality. A thing that has no reality cannot be seen as real. If we have this clear comprehension of ourselves, we can practice Dharma but then we fall aprey to business and forget Dharma. One talks about Dharma or meditation while doing business, it is not better way. It is not that sitting and closing eyes means meditation but withdrawing oneself from all belongings only leads to meditation. Neither should we think that practising Dharma means you have to ordain and live in a monastery. When one is doing business or house work it is same as with the breath – one need not set aside time for these and one breathes every time as breathing is critical to life and we cannot do without it even for minutes. So seeing the frailty of our life through seeing the breath is the meditation or the recollection of death which comes when breathing stops. Just reaching this fact that if the breath goes but does not go out again or goes out and does not come in again our life is over. This should be enough to change our mind. Further, if we take interest in our breath, set mindfulness on it, many kinds of wisdoms will arise. It is easy because we all breathe. When we lie down we fix attention on it until we fall asleep. It will make the mind clear and peaceful.

Meditation is something to help us get beyond suffering. We can see what is right or wrong but if we do not practise we do not see clearly. So whatever we do we should do it with knowledge. This is how we should live. Further, if we wish to practise Dharma and live according to Dharma, we should look at nature. There are big and small trees. When dry season comes, the leaves fall and when rain comes the leaves appear again. Similarly we also dissolve and grow according to time. That is the universal truth. We are born, we age and die and take birth again like the trees and leaves. But in the case of trees, what are the causes and conditions of their existence. It is the soil and water that nourish them. For humans, it is karma which means action, which causes us to be strong or weak, to have little or more wisdom. Trees have season to grow and fall, humans have karmas. Doing good actions, things become good; doing harm, the results are painful. This truth of the existence of beings is called karma. Whatever we do is as per karmas. Practising meditation and listening to teachings, is a root cause, creating the source and making positive karmas. For listening to Dharma, there needs to be understanding. If the understanding is great, the fruits will be great and if the understanding is little, the fruits will be little too. With much right view suffering will vanish and tranquillity will come about. Again if we see according to the law of nature, it can be said that we are practising Dharma. We see that we humans are not different and the belonging to a village, country, race etc. hardly matters. In the beginning all are born, in the middle there is change and in the end we disappear from this world. It is the same for absolutely every one.

When we work we have to know the time and occasion continuing to look here will cause the mind to turn over. If it does not turn over, we cannot see Dharma. Also there must be causes. Things arise from causes. When we make efforts to practise Dharma, we are creating causes. For example a husband and wife live together. They experience love as well as disagreements and quarrels. If one of them dies, leaving the other alone, where there was a loving couple, now there is only one. That person will most probably go to find a monastery. Like people who are sick – when an illness happens, they will immediately think about finding a doctor. If they are not sick, they do not have such an idea. Things that happen then are called the causes.

Likewise in practising Dharma, we are supposed to contemplate to the point where we develop world-weariness and detachment but we cannot do it. Our meditation is similar. There can be knowledge and delusion. If there is knowledge, delusion ceases and vice versa. We, therefore, constantly contemplate birth, ageing, illness or death, which are nothing but causes. Speaking about death leads to detachment and dispassion in regard to this life. If we keep on investigating this point, entering deeper and deeper in to it, weariness with the world and detachment will come. Investigating Dharma, we will eventually see Dharma, meaning the truth and when we see Dharma, we will be able to find peace. This is the course, the meditation called establishing mindfulness on the body or contemplating the body. From the top of the head to the soles of the feet, back again from the feet to the top of the head, over and over again, we have to meditate like this to give rise to weariness and dispassion to make the mind turn over. If we are comfortable at home, the mind is not likely to turn but when we are not comfortable we think of leaving home.

When we meditate on this and really see the truth of it, the result will come by itself. When we really make up our mind through having seen impermanence, suffering and absence of a self in this body, we are called ones who have contemplated the Dharma and who are practising Dharma. What to talk of the home or universe even our skeleton cannot follow us. Then we certainly do not need to consider family, friends, wealth and possessions reliable, starting from our very bones there is nothing genuine. The only thing that is real is that which leads us to the various states of becoming and birth, meaning good and bad deeds of body, speech and mind. Doing good, brings good and acting in unwholesome ways brings pain. This only is certain and true and only this. Now having given up wrong doings, the mind is composed and can attain Samadhi and when the mind is composed in Samadhi Thusthe wisdom will born and mind will be able to contemplate things and know them as they are. Thus hearing Dharma and contemplating Dharma, pure morality and the rest arises and this is the path when hearing the name of Dharma, we do not get the idea that it is anything other than nature, we have it and are it. Therefore, the practitioners of Dharma need to investigate their feelings of attachment and aversion towards people and they occur and continuously make efforts to train our minds. Then we shall reach a place where there are no causes, where causes are exhausted. If still there is love or hate, it would mean causes exist and if there is a cause, there shall be result too. That is how it is now for us, if we go to Heavenly state we will also end up going to Hell and going to Hell we then go to Heaven. This is like becoming and birth. We should make efforts, train the mind with skilful means to make it pliable, first as a blacksmith heats metal to soften it and can then shape it into useful tool he desired. So we soften our minds with training in precepts, with restraint, with the practice of meditation and with investigation. Our minds will then soften and surrender to become peaceful.

Our practice of Dharma is to work at removing desire, aversion and delusion, the mental afflictions that can be found within each and every one of us. They are what hold us in the round of becoming and birth and prevent us from achieving peace of mind.

Therefore, realisation of peace involves working not only with the mind but with the body and the speech as well. In Dharma practice, we aim to pacify and purify the mind, but it is difficult to do, so we have to work with external control of body and speech.

In Dharma practice we aim to pacify and purify the mind, but it is difficult to do. So we have to begin with externals, body and speech working our way inward until we reach that which is smooth and resplendent. We can compare it with the finished piece of furniture such as a chair or a table. These may be attractive now but once they were just rough bits of wood with branches and leaves that had to be planned and worked. This is the way we get furniture that is beneficial or the mind that is perfect and pure. Therefore, the right path to peace for attaining true happiness is morality, Samadhi and wisdom. This is path of practice. It is way to complete abandonment of craving attachment, aversion and confusion. This path involves going against our habitual tendencies of taking it easy and wanting enjoyment and comfort so we have to be ready to endure some difficulty and put forth effort.

If the mind is able to look after itself, it is not so difficult to guard speech and bodily actions since they are motivated and supervised by the mind, as it is mind where the intention for all our actions originates. If we are mindful, we will see the objects that pass in to the mind and our reactions thereto. The one who knows will automatically take them up as objects of contemplation. That aspect of discerning the good from the bad and the right from the wrong from among all phenomena in our field of awareness is wisdom. This is the wisdom in its initial stage and it matures as the practice progresses. This is the way morality meditation and wisdom is practised in the beginning. We have to continue to practice like this as much as possible and we might even reach a point where we are constantly judging and finding fault with every one we meet. We constantly react with attractions and aversions to the world around us becoming full of all kinds of uncertainties and continually attaching to views about how to practise. It is as if we have become obsessed with the practice. But it is still better to continue practice and practice a lot and dedicate to looking after body, speech and mind which can never be done too much. Once we have a foundation, there will be a strong sense of shame and fear of wrong doing established in the heart, whatever the time and place, in public or in private, we will not want to do anything that is harmful to us or to others. The practice of mindfulness and restraint with body, speech and mind and the consistent distinguishing between right and wrong is what we hold as a focus. As the mind becomes more refined, mindfulness becomes more focussed. The practice actually becomes easier as the mind turns more and more inward to focus on itself. We no longer make big mistakes or deviate wildly and the end result is that we can clearly see the mind and its objects without having to make any distinction between mind, body and speech. We find that the body depends on the mind in order to function and as we continue to turn inward and wisdom matures, eventually we are left contemplating the mind and its object – which means we start to experience the body as something immaterial.

So the purpose of practice is to seek inwardly, investigating until we reach the original mind which is pure and without attachment. It is not affected by mental objects and does not chase after pleasant and unpleasant phenomena. Rather it is in a state of continuous wakefulness, thoroughly aware of all its experiences. When the mind is like this, it does not become anything and nothing can shake it because there is awareness seeing that all things are merely conditions arising out of the confluence of the elements without any individual controlling them. In the past because of the roots of desire, aversion and delusion already existed in the mind, whenever we caught sight of the slightest pleasant or unpleasant things, the mind would react immediately. The mind itself is actually free but we had to suffer because of our attachment. That is how it is as long as the mind does not know itself as long as it is not illumined, it is not free, it is influenced by whatever phenomena it experiences it is without a refuge and is so unable to truly depend on itself although original mind is beyond good or bad.

# Chapter XIV

## Samadhi

Coming to Samadhi, it means a mind that is firmly concentrated and the more we practise the firmer it becomes. The more we contemplate, the more confident we become. It becomes easier to know the arising and passing away of consciousness from moment to moment. The mind becomes truly stable to the point when it cannot be swayed by anything at all and we are absolutely confident that no phenomena, whatsoever, have the power to shake it. The mind experiences good or bad mental states, happiness and suffering, because it is deluded by its objects and the objects of mind are the objects of mind and the mind is the mind. If the mind is not deluded by them, there is no suffering. The undeluded mind cannot be shaken. This is the state of awareness in which all phenomena are viewed entirely as elements arising and passing away. This state that has arisen in the mind itself , if we contemplate according to the truth the things are, we will see that only one path existed and there was nothing else to do in life but follow it. Attaching to either happiness or suffering will cause suffering to arise.

If we understand this and are mindful with the right view, we are not yet able to fully let go of our attachment. So we must walk the middle path which means being aware of the various states of happiness and suffering, while at the same time keeping them at a distance. As whenever the mind attaches to the state of happiness and suffering, awareness of the attachment is there. We do not encourage or give value to the positive state even as we are holding on to them and we do not despise or fear the negative states. This way we can observe the mind as it actually is and at all times we take the middle way of equanimity as the object of mind and more along the path little by little. When eventually the mind is fully aware of the various positive and negative states, it is able to lay aside the happiness and suffering, the pleasure and sadness, to lay aside all that is the world and so become the knower of the world. The mind in full knowing can then let go and settle down for the reason that we have done the practice and followed the path to this point. We know what we must do to reach the end of the path and we keep striving to uproot and dislodge our attachments and when there is attachment to happy or unhappy states of mind, there must be the clear and unwavering understanding that any such attachment is attachment to the world, being stuck in the world which is created and established through ignorance. The mind still follows various states of joy and sorrow but does not get completely lost in them. We sustain a continuous effort to destroy any attachment in the mind to clear from the mind all that is the world. Once the mind is practising this and experiencing this, it does not have to go following up on or searching for anything else. Instead it will be aware of whatever arises with full mindfulness. The mind and phenomena are just as they are and the mind is not creating anything additional. So we should keep practising, claiming the mind little by little and if we start thinking, it does not matter, if we are not thinking, it does not matter. The important thing is to develop this understanding of the mind.

What we, however, see is that among all groups of people, if people have happy lives, they will not be very interested in these things and it is usually the old and the infirm who feel interested in it. It is the old ones who want to keep precepts. Modern-minded people do not see anything of value here. That is why, we, in our society have increased trouble, conflict and distress. It is just because we lack morality. There is no honesty or integrity and when everyone becomes like this, there can be only heat and torment. When honesty and integrity are gone, we can say they are about half gone. So we can see there is a lot of turmoil and strife in many places. The reason for this is that morality and Dharma are lost to people and the pursuit of pleasure and excitement has taken their place and it happens like this. Morality and Dharma are true and correct. There is nothing incorrect in them. A poor person can practise the path of God. A life that is established on a foundation of goodness will shine brilliant and supreme. We need not worry that any good we do will be wasted. Even after we die, the virtue we have created will remain in the world. Our children will carry it on and when others meet our children or see anything that was connected with us they will think about us and feel happy. In this way we are still giving refuge and assistance to others in the world.

If we do not have Dharma in our lives, we are no different from animals. The animals, like us, eat, sleep and breed. If we raise an animal, we go on caring for it and the animal thinks we love it. But when it grows up it is sold in the market for some pennies. So where is love, it is only for our pleasure we bring it up and when it has reached our expectations we sell it. Even when the animal is put for being chucked off, it is smeared and messaged. It still feels enjoyed but after that it is chucked off. So we human beings love to be happy and selfish only having no Dharma and if we do not have Dharma, but live by envy and ill-will, society will have no peace or happiness. Morality, therefore, is a treasure. All wealth and enjoyment is born of morality. There is the treasure of wealth, the treasure of eyes, ears, nose, tongue, body and mind. All these things that we possess as we sit here are treasures and accomplishments and they are born of past moral conduct, the treasure of morality and when we think of treasure we only think about the kinds of wealth that can be seen by the eyes, such as money, possessions, jewels etc. We do not consider our own eyes and ears themselves. If these limbs and senses are not whole, how can we enjoy material riches? If someone wants to purchase our eyes, we cannot give for any value. Therefore, the riches have no value before the organs and the organs have no value before the Dharma, which teaches complete detachment from these. Thus it is morality which is parent of all Dharma as the breath is the progenitor of all our limbs and organs. If the breath stops we cannot continue to function and our limbs are in vain. So above all belongings and limbs and body it is morality of Dharma which is precious and should be practised. If people were to practice and realise this for themselves, the truth penetrates their hearts that would be the most excellent sort of merit. People should, therefore, genuinely understand and practice Dharma like that even if we have all the conceptual knowledge.

# Chapter XV

## Meditation Practice – Part of Dharma

Now coming to the meditation practice, we have all been practising meditation for a while but still we are not sure about the practice yet. Making the mind peaceful is known as Samadhi (Concentration) meditation. Mind is extremely changeable and unreliable. Sometimes we sit for meditation and in no time at all mind is calm and other days no matter what we do there is no calm. The mind constantly struggles to get away. Some days it goes well and some days it is awful. We are usually taught to close our eyes in sitting meditation so that we are not busy looking at external things. With eyes closed our attention is naturally turned inward towards the mind, the source of many different kinds of knowledge. Sitting with the eyes not focussed on any external object, we should establish awareness with the breath. By keeping with it, we will come to know the place that is the focal point of awareness and when the factors of path are at work together, we will be able to see our breath, feelings, mind and mental objects as they are in the present moment. Ultimately we will know that place that is both the focal point of Samadhi and the unification of the path factor. When developing Samadhi, we should fix our attention on the breath and imagine that we are sitting alone with no other people and nothing else around to bother us. We should develop this perception, sustaining it until the mind completely lets go of the world outside, and all that is left is simply the awareness of the breath entering and leaving. The mind must set aside the external world and we should not think of the people sitting around us; should not allow thoughts that may stir in mind. It would be better if they are thrown out. Then we can fix our attention solely on the in and out breaths. We should then allow the breath to continue normally and smoothly and observe it entering and leaving the body. Once the mind is out of the external objects, we will no longer feel disturbed by the sound of traffic or other noises. We would not feel irritated with anything outside because the mind would not be paying attention to them as it becomes centred up on the breath. Still if the mind is agitated by different things and we are not able to concentrate, we should take an extra deep breath until the lungs are completely full and then release all the air until there is none left inside. If we do it several times we will be able to re-establish awareness and continue to develop concentration. Having re-established mindfulness, it is normal that for a period the mind would be calm and then it might be distracted again. So when it happens we have to bring it back again and again. Once the mind has become concentrated, we should maintain awareness at that point where it is focussed. Then we shall see the breath clearly as it enters and leaves. Mindfulness shall be sharp and awareness of mental objects and mental activity shall be clearer. At that point we will be able to see the characteristics of concentration or Samadhi and wisdom and the way they merge together. Once this unification of path factors occurs, our mind shall be free from all sorts of turbulences. It will become one-pointed and this is Samadhi. At this stage we should make the mind unshakable in its concentration and be especially mindful.

As we continue to practice, we should understand that there is nothing to worry about. We should feel relaxed and unworried securely in the mind. Once the mind is concentrated one-pointed, nothing shall be able to penetrate or disturb it and we shall be able to sit like this for as long as we wished. Having developed Samadhi to this level we will be able to enter and leave at will without any hindrance. Receiving the results of Samadhi like this has a purifying effect on the mind.

This is where the practice actually begins and it is the fruit that comes as Samadhi matures. Greater purity of conduct facilitates the development of stronger and more refined Samadhi and this in turn supports the maturing of wisdom and in the end these terms become synonymous. As these factors continue to mature together, they form one complete circle giving rise to the "path" which is the synthesis of these three functions of practice working smoothly and consistently together. We should preserve this energy which will give rise to the special insight. Having reached this stage when wisdom functions in the mind independent of whether the mind is tranquil or not, wisdom shall provide a consistent energy in our practice. We then will have no attachments with outside world and then the heart shall feel much lighter and the mind shall remain peaceful.

Now there are two kinds of peacefulness. One is the peace that comes through Samadhi and the other is the peace that comes through wisdom. The mind that is peaceful through Samadhi is still deluded as such peace is dependent upon the mind being separated from phenomena. When it does not experience any contact or activity, there shall be calm and consequently we shall get attached to the happiness that comes with that calm state. But as soon as there is infringement through the senses, the mind gives in right away. It gets afraid of phenomena. It will be afraid of happiness and suffering; of praise and criticism; afraid of forms, sounds, smells, tastes etc. People who are peaceful through Samadhi alone are afraid of everything and do not want to get involved with anybody or anything because they are afraid that their state of mind shall be disturbed. People practising this way just want to stay in isolation to experience the bliss of Samadhi without having to leave it. They want to hide themselves away in a quiet place. When we have contemplated sufficiently, it is alright to establish Samadhi. We can re-enter it through sitting meditation and then with calm re-established, continue with the contemplation using the state of calm to train and purify the mind as well as to challenge it. As we gain knowledge, we should use it to combat the mental afflictions as if we simply enter Samadhi and stay there. We do not gain any insight but making the mind calm only. However, if we use the calm mind to reflect, beginning with our external experience, this calm will gradually penetrate deeper and deeper inward until the mind experiences the most profound peace of all.

On the other hand the peace that comes through wisdom is distinctive because when the mind withdraws from tranquillity, the presence of wisdom makes it unafraid of sights, sounds, smells, tastes, physical sensations and thoughts. It means that as soon as there is sense contact, the mind is immediately aware of what is happening. When there is contact, we should lay it aside because our mindfulness is sharp enough to let it go the right way. When we train the mind like this, it becomes considerably more refined than when we develop Samadhi alone. With such energy gained by mind we become fearless. This is power of meditation and when such a quality of awareness arises within our mind, the practice can be called meditation, clearly knowing in accordance with the truth. This is the peace at the highest level. Once we recognise this, we shall be developing awareness at all times and in all postures. If the mind is thus restrained and composed with uninterrupted mindfulness, we shall know the wholesome and unwholesome mental state that arises and wherever we go, we will be practising.

If we train the mind in this way our meditation shall mature quickly and successfully. There can be so many problems but we have to be aware that anything can happen in Samadhi but we should not mind as such are only impermanent mental functions. There is no inherent reality in these otherwise these could make us very confused and there will be no end to it. We should fix our attention on whatever arises and watch it pass away. This would give us a foundation to be more firm in our conviction of mindful awareness and meditation. You will also find some people practising very comfortably. They do not have obstructions and there is no suffering for them. This is previous karma coming to fruition in the present life. When the mind becomes concentrated, this karma rushes in and invades which does not necessarily mean occurrence of bad experiences. They can be happy experiences also making the mind bright and clear. However, all experiences are a peril to the mind and we should not get fixated on them at all. The important point is to have mindfulness in all situations and mindfulness is to be aware of the way the things are. But things can still appear as right and wrong; there can still be feeling of like and dislike but we should just keep letting them go with the recognition that they are impermanent.

We can come to know the source of things and reach the place that is called original mind when nothing is permanent, when nothing is anything at all and that is the Truth. Further, Samadhi has its difficulties as we can get side-tracked. When we sit, we have no many experiences. We see light, colours and we get caught up in all these but it is really like a child fascinated by animals and asking endless questions. That is what a child has to do because he does not know what the things are and when he grows up he would know and would put no more questions. We should, therefore, put such questions and doubts away from our mind and that actually is the mindfulness. We should recognise whatever appears to mind as merely a moment of sensation and awareness, something impermanent that arises and passes away. There is nothing more than that. There is no self or other, no essence and nothing should be grasped therefrom. When body and mind are seen thus with wisdom, we are aware of all the old habits and patterns but seeing the impermanence of mind and body; seeing the impermanence of the totality of all feelings of happiness and suffering, of love and hate, we realise there is only so much to them that they are merely what they are and the mind turns away from them. What we should do is to make earnest efforts in the things we do but our actions should not be mixed with desires. They should be performed with the aim of letting go and realising non-attachment. We do what we need to do but with letting go the ideas otherwise occurring to our mind.

People in the world do whatever they do to get something - like the people who come to see us in our capacity as doctors and administrators, it is because they want something. Generally whatever is done because of a wish to get something and attachment and clinging to things becomes a way of life. But we should continue doing our work according to our responsibilities. If we act like this doing work that is correct with right understanding, we would be at ease and if we think according to Dharmas, we can come to have ease of mind, gradually tracking ourselves. We plant a mango tree with the desire to get fruit but will every mango be edible? When we enjoy ripe mangoes we do not consider how many were lost or rejected. If we get discouraged by considering this, we might not like to plant the tree in the first place. Many of the mangoes fall and rot before they are ripe; some fall and some we will have to throw away but we still plant and take care of the trees. We can eat mangoes thinking that it is like this only. We want to plant fruit trees when the mangoes just fall off permanently and we may not be able to eat mangoes at all. So we have to act discarding the impermanent ideas and still working on whatever the good understanding is and thinking that in Samadhi, wisdom and awareness we are guided by the permanency leaving aside the impermanent.

Seeing all this, we feel Dharma is something difficult and it is troublesome but if we really contemplate it, it would be something that could make an end of our problems. The things are, therefore, not impossible to practice. Among all the things that which are being practised by people, do not exist. Therefore, we own only those which benefit us and benefit others. Things that are of no benefit to us and others should be let off. Further, if suffering occurs in our daily life we should consider why that is happening. It might be that our children do not listen to us. But who made these children. If we suffer because of our children, actually the cause resides in us only. We have to think like this returning to the origin and if we want to try to fix the situation by forcing them to be a certain way, it would be beyond our means. We will not be able to accomplish it and will end up in tears over our children. In truth there is a cause and a reason. We have to pay attention and see what it is. Things do not just bubble up and appear without cause but we do not really search it out very seriously. The world is like this. Usually people come to recognise this because nature has ripened for them they have had a lot of experiences. Then they may hear a little of Dharma and they look back with great regret for having suffered for so many years. Still if we do not ignore the same and keep clinging to it there would be no peace throughout our lives. Things are cast in a certain way and if we want to be otherwise, we shall have to see the phenomena of truth and that is all.

We may sometimes feel that living at home is troublesome, but when we leave for a while, we start to feel home sick. It is because when we go somewhere, we do not really reach the place of satisfaction, our thinking does not get them as no place is enjoyable and pleasant as home for us. It means that the business of good or bad is not finished yet and we do things in a worldly way and if it is not finished, we have not put things down and if we have not put them down, we still carry them and carrying them, we feel heaviness and we see the fault of it. We then have to come down to practising patient endurance.

This world is Loka, means darkness. However much the world processes and develops, darkness develops just that much – people talk enthusiastically about how the world is progressing but it is only darkness spreading. In the past when there were no toilets built in houses, people used to go to ease in forests. This made them walk and go out in fresh air but after constructing toilets in home they need not go out at all leading to no physical exercise besides incurring lot of expenditure and then we feel we do not have enough money to go by. Even if we have sufficient money, we do not consider it enough as the demand for money goes on increasing. We should earn our living in a way that is right livelihood and make good use of it conserving it for meaningful ends. Whatever we may need, we should not let it go to excess but whatever we see others getting, we want to match them and for this we are always in want of money however much we may earn. This leads to our suffering. We say it is for this or that reason but we never point at source. The root is in not having enough and we find out the reason elsewhere.

If we put effort in to cleaning up our minds, the way we do sweeping our houses, washing and scrubbing our clothes also, we would likely be at ease but when we talk about cleansing like this, people do not know what we are getting at. It is just like someone being indifferent to whether the dishes are clean or dirty. It is an ignorant type of indifference. We have to go to work and clean, otherwise we never reach the correct point and the mind remains in this befouled, ignorant condition. For the most part things are imitation. We grasp these things that are false and uncertain as real but we should see that which is not false but genuine. For this we have to turn inward to see. If the mind does not see and realise, there is no path to clarify. We have to therefore, turn up our mind to realise the real from the false. This is like someone riding a motorcycle loses control and falls down. He will say the motorcycle made him fall but actually he made the motorcycle fall because he could not drive it well. Therefore, one has to learn the right from the wrong but if someone knows and still does not act accordingly, he can never be set right. We should, therefore, have willingness to be set right.

We are practitioners of Dharma and all Dharmas are nature, existing as it is. Nature is exclusively and completely Dharma. These things are not yet clear to us because we have not come to know the way to practice so we need to rely on the instructions and training of a qualified teacher. Nature also teaches us things such as trees are born from their causes and grow accordingly. This we can learn from trees but we do not. We do not see them as something for us to turn inward and reflect upon. We should know that Dharma is the tree teaching us but we do not realise that yet. The trees give fruit. We eat without any real investigation or consideration. Sweet and sour tastes are their nature, these characteristics are Dharma and the fruit are teaching us something but we do not understand them. Similarly when the leaves of the trees wither and die, they fall. We only see leaves falling, we do not realise this is Dharma like one has to born, give fruit and then die. The leaves of the trees fall and the new bush appears. We see the cycle but we do not think much about it that is the cycle of the beings to be born and die. For this we have to turn inward and see that our own birth and death are not so very different from that of tree.

This body comes into being as a result of various causes and depends on the five elements for its existence. It grows and comes to fruition of different kinds just like a tree and falling leaves and new buds are no different from the lives of the people. When we understand this we have learnt Dharma. After understanding Dharma we will strive to see Dharma everywhere and in all things to see the characteristics of our five ingredients that are in a continually state of flux, moving, changing and transforming without any let up. Whether we are studying, sitting, walking or lying down, we employ mindfulness to guard and watch all times. Seeing external things, it is the same as seeing internal phenomena and seeing internal phenomena is the same as seeing external phenomena because they are of the same nature. One who has understood it is awakened.

# Chapter XVI

## Misconceptions and Mistaken Practices

We are down with many misconceptions and mistaken practices of ordinary beings being immersed in the pursuit of pleasure, comfort and happiness in the pride that seeks to elevate and extol ourselves, is not the path that one who has gone forth from the world shall walk the state of dis-satisfaction and suffering of negativity, aversion, anger and self-mortification. It brings about no benefit at all. All worldly beings are consistently in search of happiness and pleasure. They are habituated to the extreme reactions of allocation and aversion to things and are always being bounced back and forth between the two as they undergo ceaseless change and keep on trading places. This is the way of the world. If there is happiness there will be suffering too. These are the things that will always be uncertain. Thus they are the Dharmas of those who are mired in the world, those who are not at peace. Those who are at peace do not go this way but they do see and know about these things. They see pleasure and happiness but do not accept them as real, they do not get attached to or stuck in them. They are aware of whatever aversions there may be to things but they do not take that as a path either. These are the people who see the path. Those who are tranquil understand the way that is not tranquil while still remaining at peace. The way of seeking happiness with its resultant depression and elation over things is recognised as a mistaken path. The wise also experience such phenomena but do not expect to find any ultimate meaning in them. So they do not mind such reactions. The ones who are at peace are mistaken by these things by happiness and suffering. When there is no more meaning seen in things one naturally lets go the happiness and suffering in accord with their nature. When happiness and suffering are known for what they are, they become invalid phenomena. They have no meaning in the mind of the weakened being. There is mere recognition of them that happiness and suffering are appearing like hot and cold, it is not that there is no recognition or awareness, like the water in contact with the lotus but cannot penetrate or submerge it. The afflictions are like the water and the mind of the practitioner is lotus leaf. It merely recognises these states but they cannot penetrate the mind. This means that there is no grasping and no attachment to things. In Dharma, it is called equanimity i.e. keeping the mind balanced and neutral.

Thus we should develop the path, which is wisdom. This path can be summarised as developing morality to the utmost, developing Samadhi to the utmost and developing wisdom to the utmost. These are the tools and faculties for destroying the fiction that is called the world, the path for destroying the worldliness dwelling in the hearts of deluded beings. Whenever attachment to happiness and suffering to gain and loss is present in the mind, the world is there, the mind is the world. A worldly being has been born of craving and if craving is extinguished, the world is extinguished because this blind craving is the source of the world. When we determine to practice and develop this path, we try to practice Samadhi to focus and pacify the mind. But the mind does not become focussed and peaceful so easily. We do not want it to think but it keeps on thinking. Really the mind of an ordinary person is like someone sitting on a nest of red ants, have to face the biting of the ants. When we, who have the worldly Dharmas filling our hearts, start to practice with our worldly minds, the habits of attraction and aversion, elation and depression, distraction and worry, all immediately start to surface. This is quite a natural occurrence for those who have not yet attained the Dharma and whose minds are filled with worldliness. We have not yet seen through these habits and are thus not able to resist their power. So it is just like sitting on an ant hill. But when they bite we have to find a solution to destroy them by putting down poison, putting down earth etc. so that they flee. This is what the practice entails making an effort to combat what torments us. We also learn about resisting, grating against things. The way of transcendence grates against the worldly; right view grates against wrong view; purity grates against impurity – these things are always going to be incompatible.

Further, we have impulses of desires and attractions but we do not have to crave and uproot these habits. These days most of us practitioners have little faith and devotion. We practice for a year or two and are full of desire for rapid attainments. Practising well, really training the mind and developing our qualities, we can gain experience and then we can appreciate the virtues of Dharma but it takes time depending up on how fast we become adept in these concepts of Dharma. Still the reality exists in the phenomena of nature in their appearing, chaufing and disappearing. That is their truth. It is the people who are not true. We become excited by things but phenomena are not excited in their levels. We become attached to things wanting them to be a certain way, taking them to be ours. We react with extreme emotions depending on whether they seem to turn out in the right way or wrong way, meaning whether they turn out according to our desires but whatever we encounter, it just arises and passes away. Pleasant and unpleasant phenomena still keep appearing to mind but we merely recognise their appearance. Our mind firmly established in awareness, we can no longer react to things with gladness or dejection. So we should practice Dharma that sees according to reality, wisdom knowing the truth of all existing shall be born in us. This is one who knows and sees Dharma. When one knows one renounces and let go of things which lay down the burden and when one really attains and sees there is nothing to be endured or given up. When one sees Dharma, there is only Dharma, and in Dharma, there is no enduring or renouncing. But when we do not yet know and realise Dharma, when it is not one being, we have to apply the convention of Dharma, exerting ourselves in various practices. We have to apply effort because of the tendency of laziness. We apply endurance and forbearance because of lack of determination and our inability to bear things and restrain ourselves. But if one has practised well and is habituated to it, no kind of forced effort is needed.

There is the view that the body is ours. Dharma says it is not ours and we come to yield on this point. We recognise that it is true and do not need to probe any more. Previously unsure about all phenomena, we are no longer in doubt now that we have relinquished the belief in a self. Then there is attachment to rites and rituals, behind belief in the efficacy of conventional modes of behaviour. These are connected, one leading to the other types of mental afflictions. From seeing the nature of the body and letting go, doubt disappears and when there is no doubt, there is no more groping. This applies to all the aggregates – body, feeling, perception, conceptualisation and consciousness. In such a situation whatever arises, we should pick it up, examine it and see it clearly. If we cannot yet see it for what it is, put it aside for the time and go on practising Dharma. In course of time we shall realise the reality and then the doubt shall be removed. If we keep on thinking, then we shall not be able to proceed with practising Dharma.

When mindfulness is incharge and protects us in this way, there is tranquillity in the mind which will lead to wisdom because of seeing all these things asking us to look in to it and when the mind is in a settled and awake state resulting from proper meditation, it is like a freshly swept path, as soon as a few leaves fall, we will notice them. They will be easy to see on the ground. But if the mind is not guarded or controlled, it is like a forest-floor covered with leaves and if a few more leaves fall, they are lost amongst those already on the ground. Further, wisdom grows as we see the nature of phenomena. We see there is no way to solve, undo or adjust things. We should accept the transitory nature of existence, accept things as they are and the result shall be peace. Suffering is then quelled because of this surrender and acceptance. When we surrender, clinging attachment is uprooted and we see there is really nothing there, there is nothing left. We have perceptions of self and others, beings, people and so forth, but in fact these are only conventions, appearances and in ultimate transcendent reality there is nothing. The body we perceive is only a coming together of the five elements. Men and women are like that. Everyone is actually like that. All are the same and seeing this leads to a state of ease. For example, we are taught to meditate on the food we eat. Looking at it and contemplating properly, we can see there is nothing really special, not a whole lot. There is the food and there is us, the two parts that are just the elements and then they get put together. That is it. We will not then get too worked up over our food now but if we cannot see it like this and if we cannot accept that this is all there is food, we will suffer. The person who accepts that the food and the person who eats it are the same mere combination of elements will have lightness but for the person who cannot accept, there is heaviness.

So dwelling in right view, we will be at peace, no matter where we are. Actually when good people try to practise, it will make them mad and all kinds of sufferings and turmoils flair up. Mind filled with pride, wandering all over, always wanting things to be other than they were. Everything was always too big or too small, too long or too short. Nothing was ever right.

There was no moderation and no middle ground. It was outside the natural balance of Dharma, always in a condition of struggle, we have to practise to stop this insanity in order to feel better. It is the salvation only which leaves us beyond becoming and birth. People do not understand this. They only understand matters of becoming and birth. If there is no becoming, there is no place to live and if there is no place to live, what shall we do. Ordinary people think it is better to stay here. They want to be born again but they do not want to die. But this cannot be as this only causes problems. People think like this because they do not understand unsatisfactoriness of life. I want to be born but I do not want to die. It boils down no more than this as death comes from birth and if we do not want to die, we will not be able to born. Speaking with people who are under the sway of desire and attachment it is difficult and getting them to the point of letting go will really be hard. Defilement and craving are like that. If there is no place to set a pillar, how can we talk about building something that is like no becoming and birth, no place to be born but when we talk about this, people will not listen and understand. When talking about self, it is emphatically pointed out that there is no such thing.

Self is only a convention and on the absolute level, the level of liberation, it does not exist. There is just elemental nature arising only for the reason that causes and conditions are manifesting. We suppose that this is self arising, and we grasp at it. When there is this supposition, we grasp at 'me' and then there is 'mine' arising together with it but we do not even know how this has taken place. So people say things like "I want to be born but I do not want to die". This is something to be known within ourselves and we can tell others about it. Dharma has only pointed to us the way and further such a thing is to be realised by each individual. There are two extremes. We lean towards either side but we do not like to stay in the middle. The middle is the lonely way. Where there is attraction, we go that way. Where there is aversion, we go that way. Putting them down is lonely. We refuse to go there, but neither extreme is the way of one who is tranquil. We, therefore, need to be free of pleasure and pain, for neither is the way of peace. Once free of these things we can be peaceful. With no more attachment and giving meaning of things, there is no need for any more doing. It is the state of peace. Things arise and we come to realise they are not certain. This is not real, that is not real. Where is the real right there? In brief this is like this and that is like that is not right. Let the things go on, we should put down the judging and guessing. We go back and forth passing it by again and again and we are always in the state of suffering. Therefore, we should end our doubts and stop thinking making an end of it right here.

We practice Dharma to know nature and allow it to go according to its condition, ofcourse it is talking about the material world. As to the mind it cannot be left to follow its own conditions, it has to be trained. Now born in to this world we all have afflictions of desire, anger and delusion. Desire makes us crave various things and causes the mind to be in a state of imbalance and turmoil. That can only lead to torment and distress. It is therefore better to train it in Dharma, in Truth. When aversion occurs in us we want to express anger towards people and it may get to the point of physically attacking or even killing someone. But we do not just let the impulse go according to its nature.

We see it for what it is and teach the mind about it. This is practising Dharma. Delusion is the same. When it happens, we are confused about things. If we merely have it as it is, we remain in ignorance. So we have to learn about nature to train the mind to know exactly what nature is. People are born with physical form and mind. In the beginning these things are born, in the middle they change and in the end they are extinguished. This is the nature. We cannot do much to alter these facts. We train our minds as we can and when the time comes, we have to let go of it all. It is not in the power of humans to change this or get beyond it. The Dharma is something to be applied while we are here for making actions, words and thoughts correct and are wholesome. We, therefore, have to transcend the world, not be prisoners to worldly ways and habits. Dharma teaches us self, about the concept of self and that the things are not really self. We attach to things and invest them with meaning. When we do this we cannot disentangle from this. The involvement deepens and this mess gets worse and worse. If we know that there is no self, the body and mind are really not self and when we keep on investigating, we will eventually come to realise the actual condition of selflessness. We will genuinely see that there is no self and other pleasure is merely pleasure. Feeling is merely feeling and thinking is merely thinking.

# Chapter XVII

## Realisation of Selflessness

When the realisation of selflessness comes to full measure, we will be able to relate to the things of this world to our most cherished possessions and involvements, to friends and relations, wealth, accomplishments and status, just as we do to our clothes. When clothes are new, we wear them, they get dirty and we wash them and after some time they are worn out and we discard them. Thus we are constantly getting rid of the old things and starting to use new garments. We will have the exactly same feeling about our existence in the universe. We will not moan or cry over things, we will not be tormented or burdened by them. They will remain the same as they were before but our feelings towards and understanding of them gets changed. Our knowledge will be exalted and we will see truth.

So we should take the Dharma as our foundation, our basis. Living and practising in the world, we will take ourselves, our ideas, desires and opinions as basis. Taking ourselves as our standard, we are merely infatuated with that person. Being enthralled with ourselves or with another is not the way of Dharma. Dharma does not incline to any individual or follow personalities. It follows the truth. It does not simply accord with the likes and dislikes of people as such habitual reactions have nothing to do with the truth. If we really consider all of this and investigate thoroughly, we will enter the correct path. We are suffering because of lack of knowledge, not knowing where things begin and end; not understanding the cause, this is ignorance and when there is this ignorance, various desires arise and driven by them, we create the causes of suffering. Then the result must be suffering. This is origination itself. If we understand these things, morality will be born within us and Dharma too shall be born. We need not have too many concerns and anxieties.

Just look within, look at the place without desires, the place without anger and there shall be no delusion. Then when the breath ends and we die, no matter through how many life times, if the causes for becoming and birth still exist, the consciousness is likely to try and take birth in a place it is familiar with. Karma drives beings in to their various births. They cycle back and forth through the round of births, just changing appearance, appearing with a different face next time but we do not recognise it. We are just coming and going and returning in the round of Sansara, really just remaining where we are.

Arjuna, reluctant to fighting, had been arguing with Krishna, the various aspects, who could lead him to believe that what he thought was not correct thing for him and the correct thing to do was to fight and this was his karma as Kshatriya as also his Dharma. He so far had lacked Dharma, which could lead him to resort to his karma i.e. fighting. Krishna wants an assurance from him that he was all in all and everything of the world and all gods were within him. He should, therefore, have full credence in whatever he told. Such faith only, till direct realisation came, would enable the being to strictly follow the advice and never swerve from the Dharma that would be shown to him. This advice is the direct realisation and is certain and beyond doubt and who are lacking in such faith to follow the advice are led away by their limited intelligence. The secret advice, which Krishna is going to impart, is so incomprehensible and contrary to the common experience of the generality of beings that it joins with their reason and intelligence and was likely to be cavilled at by the most. There, therefore, has to be uncavilling nature and faith as the essential conditions for the revelation of the supreme secret.

The whole universe is pervaded by him, who is of unmanifest form and all things rest in him and not that he rested in them. Even the beings did not rest in him but he only is the cause of all beings. Therefore, he was in a capacity to guide and advise him the correct path and action to be adopted in the situation in which he had despised himself. First thing is He is there everywhere and He cannot be divided into parts. He, therefore, pervades in whole universe. He only rests in Akash, Vayu, moving everywhere and all beings rest in Him. He, by the help of his own Prakriti, sends forth again and again the whole multitude of beings, helpless from being ruled by Prakriti. All actions of Prakriti did not bind Him and He rests indifferent-like unattached to those actions. He directs Prakriti to give birth to the moving and the unmoving and because of this only the universe revolves. People, however, deluded in human body hopes in vain and do actions in vain due to vain knowledge, devoid of Chitta. Such people are only of Rakshashik and Asurik Prakriti. The wise persons, however, refuged in Daivi prakriti, as against the Rakshashik Prakriti, with Manas resting on none other are considered to be devoted to Him, knowing Him as the origin of beings and immutable. Such persons worship Him ever harmonised and with full devotion and firm in their vow and others worship Him by Gyan and Vigyan are devoted to Him, the all faced, in manifold ways as unity and as diversity. The knowers of the Vedas, who worshipped Him by Yajna, pray for a passage to the Swarga Loka, attain the righteous world of the Lord of gods, partake in Heaven of the celestial enjoyments of gods and having enjoyed that extensive Heaven would, their Punyas exhausted, enter the world of mortals.

Thus the followers of Dharma obtain going and coming but the men who meditated exclusively on Him are devoted to Him, the wants and well-being of those, the ever-harmonised are taken care of by Him alone. The devotees of even other gods, who worship them with full faith, they too worship Him only, though irregularly. But such people do not know him in essence and hence they fall.

He accepts even a leaf, a flower, a fruit, even water if offered with devotion. Therefore, whatever one eats, does action, does Yajna etc., one should dedicate that to Him only. Even if a person of very evil ways devoted to Him and none other, he is deemed to be righteous too as he is rightly resolved and soon such a person becomes dutiful self and attains peace. Therefore, His devotee never perishes. Therefore, one, who takes refuge in Him, attains Supreme goal irrespective of whether he is a woman, a Vaishya or a Shudra. Here Krishna authorises women, Vaishyas and Shudras too his Bhakti. Kshatriyas and Brahmins are already authorised as such and only women, Vaishyas and Shudras were not considered at that time the Adhikaris of Bhakti. So Krishna has clarified that position even. Therefore, he asks Arjuna to have full faith in Him and be His devotee, be able to sacrifice all to Him and then he would be considered as His devotee.

Krishna has been telling Arjuna his karma as a Kshatriya on his having declined to resort to fighting after reaching the battle field in Kurukshetra. Krishna tells him the final advice in this regard as will be delighting to him and shall be for his well being. He told that his origin is not known even to the gods and the rishis and the one, who knows him the unborn, beginingless, the great Lord of the worlds and who is undeluded amongst the mortals is liberated from all sins. Therefore, intelligence, knowledge, non-delusion, forbearance, truth, sense-restraint, mental control, happiness, pain, birth, existence, fear and fearlessness, harmlessness, equanimity, contentment, austerity, gift, fame, obloquy, these various kinds of characteristics arise from Him only and the one who knows this divine power of Krishna in essence, he with unshaken Yoga, is endowed and there was no doubt in that. Arjuna should, therefore, worship Him, with his Chitta and Prana, mutually illumining and remembering Him constantly would be content and ever-enjoying. Those who constantly harmonised and worship Him with love get in turn the Budhi Yoga by which he could attain Him and he by mere mercy destroys his ignorance born darkness by the cuminons lamp of Gyana. On hearing these words of Krishna, Arjuna was convinced of His being overall Lord and desired to be told in detail, His Yoga and glory to which there is no end. Krishna told that He only is seated in the hearts of all beings. He is the beginning, middle and the end of the beings. He is Vishnu, the Sun, Marich, the Moon, the Vedas, the Vishwa and chetna of all people. He is the Shankara, Vittesh, Parake, Meru, Brihaspati (the chief of priests), Skand and Ocean and above all He is everything and there was no being, moving or unmoving, which might exist without Him. To prove this Krishna showed him His Vishal Roopa, which had not been seen by anybody but had to be shown to Arjuna with a view to convince of His reality so that he developed faith in Him and taking it that whatever He said was correct, he was required to resort to fighting. All these things could be told by a friend, guru or god. Having heard Him Arjuna was convinced that without knowing Krishna fully and for carelessness in the fondness of his love he begged to be pardoned.

Thereafter, bowing down low, with body prostrate, he implored for mercy, having now seen what he had never seen, having heard what he had never heard and having known Him and the universe which he had never known. Arjuna, having seen the gentle human form thereafter collected and restored to his former nature.

Those who centralise their Manas in Him, ever-harmonised, they worship Him with supremely endowed faith and such people are deemed by Him as the most harmonised. Such people subduing the group of their senses and keeping their Budhi balanced rejoice in the welfare of all beings and ultimately attain Him. Those, who renouncing all actions in Him taking Him as the Supreme, meditate on Him and worshipping Him with exclusive devotion are protected by Him from the ocean of this mortal world. Krishna, therefore, asks Arjuna to fix his Manas in Him, entering his Budhi also in Him and verily entering in to Him without doubt he shall attain Him and if it is not possible then at least he should take refuge in his Yoga, renunciating the fruit of all actions, undertaking self –control and with practice and Dhyana and abandoning immediate peace, he should rest in Him. Such persons devoid of hatred for all beings, friendly, compassionate, devoid of "Mineness" and "I-ness", balanced in pain and pleasure, forbearing, contented, a constant Yogi, self-controlled, resolute, with the Manas and Budhi dedicated to Him is very dear to Him. He is also dear to Him from whom the world is not agitated nor is he agitated from the world, freed from agitation of joy, jealousy, fear, desires with all undertakings renounced, who neither rejoices nor grieves nor desires, renouncing good and evil, who is full of devotion, the same to foe and friend and in honour and insult, the same in cold and heat, in pleasure and pain, free from all attachments and contented.

All this Krishna has been telling to Arjuna with a view to convince him of the duties he had to perform and for this he had to be imparted all the knowledge of Yoga etc. Here Krishna wishes to give him the Supreme knowledge, the best of all knowledge, which having known the Munis reached the supreme perfection after which they have gone from here. Having taken refuge in this knowledge, those who have attained to identify with nature are not born during evolution even nor troubled during dissolution (Pralaya). The possibility of all beings become from the germ put in the Yoni (womb) and the forms which become possible from all the Yonis, Brahma is the Great Yoni of these for which he is the seed-giver. Then the being is bound fast by the three Gunas – Sattava, Rajas and Tamas. Of these, the Sattava, luminous and healthy from its stainlessness, binds by attachment to happiness and that to the knowledge; Rajas is essence of affection and generates thirst and attachment. It binds fast the embodied by attachment to action and the Tamas is born of nescience deluding all the embodied. By inaction, heedlessness, indolence and sleep, it binds fast the embodiment. Further, Sattava attaches one to happiness, Rajas to action and Tamas unenveloping Gyan, attaches one only to inaction. Rajas and Tamas having been overcome, sattava prevails; Rajas prevails when Sattava and Tamas are overcome and Tamas prevails when Sattava and Rajas are overcome.

# Chapter XVIII

## Gyan

In all the gates in this body, when Gyan light is born, it may then be known that Sattava is on the increase. Greed, outgoing energy, initiating actions, unrest and concern – these are born in the increase of Rajas and when Tamas increases there is darkness, inertness, inaction and also delusion. When one has the predominance of Sattava and dissolution (PRALAYA) comes then he attains the spotless region of the most- wise. When one goes to dissolution in Rajas, then he is born with action attached and going to dissolution in Tamas, one is born in the yoni of deluded. The fruit of Sattava is stainless; that of Rajas it is pain and of the Tamas it is Agyan. From Sattava, Gyan is born; from Rajas, the greed and inaction; delusion and Agyan are born from Tamas. If one crosses these three Gunas, the embodied one is freed from the birth, death, old age and pain and attains immortality and is fitted to become one with Brahma. The person having been beyond the Gunas, he is devoid of pride and delusion, with the evil of attachment conquered, even intent on the self within (ADHYATMA) with desires thoroughly quietened, perfectly liberated from the pairs of opposites known as pleasure and pain, the undeluded person goes on the immutable path. Such a goal is itself the glorious splendour, the light of lights and is thus not dependent on any other light for its illumination i.e. sun, moon, fire etc. and reaches the Supreme abode. Therefore, one who is undeluded knows Him by all ingredients. This is the most secret doctrine, which has been told by Shri Krishna to Arjuna with a view to activate him from the delusion which had over-powered him and putting him to inaction. Such a person sees Him in all persons, worships Him with all organs. This should, therefore, be realised and once it is done, one is supposed to have attained everything and he is deemed to have passed beyond all delusions.

Krishna further told that one who is born with the Divine nature (DAIVA SAMPADA), he has fearlessness, purity of heart (Sattava), stability in Gyan Yoga, gift, sense-control and Yajna, study of Vedas, austerity, straightforwardness, harmlessness, veracity, angerlessness, abandonment, tranquillity, absence of calumny, compassion to beings, uncovetousness, gentleness, modesty, absence of fickleness, spiritual strength, forbearance, fortitude, purity, unmaliciousness and pridelessness. One who is born of Asuric Sampada, he comes with hypocrisy, arrogance, self-conceit, anger and insolence. Similarly the Daivi Sampada is for liberation and the Asuric is for bondage. The Daivic and Asuric Sampadas are the two streams of beings in the world. The Asuric man does not know the state of action (PRAVRITTI) and actionlessness

(NIVARITTI), nor does he know the purity nor conduct nor truth. They call the universe as truthless, basisless and Godless and originating in Kama, they produce every undesirable element. Holding this view, the lost souls of small intellect of fierce deeds come forth as enemies of the world for its destruction surrendering them to the insatiable Kama (Desire) filled with hypocrisy, self-conceit and arrogance and holding false views through delusion and of impure conduct, such people engage in their actions. Such persons are bound by hundreds of bonds of hope, given to desire and anger they strive to secure by unjust means hoards of wealth for the gratification of Kama.

Such people think that all this is gained by them to fulfil their longing and that this wealth is and shall be theirs in future. They think they have slain their enemies and can also slay others if they stood in the way of their perfection, power and enjoyment. By ignorance they delude that they are rich and well-born and none was equal to them. They fall in to the foul hell with many a fancy bewilderness, entangled in the snare of delusion and engrossed in the gratification of desires. They are self-honoured, stubborn, filled with pride and intoxication of wealth, irregularly with hypocrisy they sacrifice the normal Yajnas. Obtaining the Asuric Yoni, the deluded do not attain Him birth after birth and go to the lowest state. Such persons are destructive of the self and with desire, anger and greed, they go to Naraka and liberated from these three gates a man accomplishes the well-being of the self and thereby attains the Supreme Goal. Further, the one who setting aside the injunctions of Shastras, acts under the impulse of karma, does not attain perfection or happiness or the supreme goal. Therefore, Shastra is, perhaps, an authority for everyone in the disposition of what is ought and what is not ought to be done. Having known what is enjoined in the Shastras, it benefits him to perform action here and now.

In deciding about the propriety of or otherwise of any action, therefore, we should be guided by the authority of shastras and ought to do what they enjoin us to do. The Shastras always show the way to one's well-being, which consists in rising towards perfection and subjectivity. Arjuna being kshatriya he is and ought to be pre-eminently Rajsic, having nothing to do with any Tamas which more or less impeded the play of the Rajas and thus detracted from his Kshatriya nature and degraded him. To be a real Kshatriya, he should totally discard Tamas as to fall in to the Tamas again would mean to a Kshatriya a fall and not to rise. To rise a Kshatriya ought to advance towards Sattava and develop in to a Sattavic Brahmin. For this he should not impede his Rajas, which would mean his countenancing Tamas not by concerning himself with its course which tended towards Tamsic objectivity and not by attaching himself to the harmony of Rajas, which would mean his chaining himself to it instead of rising to the Sattava. To enable him to rise higher to the Sattava, a Kshatriya should let his Rajas its fullest play without concerning himself with its harmony or the objectivity towards which it will be coursing and he himself would always have his eye on the Sattava. The Shastras never enjoin a Kshatriya to seek fight but only that he should not avoid any fight that came to him unsought. Without being belligerent he should be brave and fearless when occasion required it. He should also not drive his Rajas but he should not stop it too as Arjuna did when he abstained. Such is the fight which the Shastras enjoined to a Kshatriya – a fight which consisted in allowing the Rajas its freest play with perfect unconcernedness in the result. Such a fight meant leaving Rajas to contribute to the universal harmony which only decided how or where it should go. It thus always righted the wrong and helped and protected the weak. Such a fight meant Dharma to a Kshatriya and not sin but universal good. Abstention from it would mean Adharma, sinning against one-self and others. The Sattavic Brahmin lived for the good of others, the Rajsic kshatriyas acted for the good of others and obeying the Shastras enjoined their respective Dharmas in accordance with the stage of evolution.

With this it will be seen that for all beings the Swabhava-born shradha became three-fold namely Sattavic, Rajsic and Tamsic. With Sattava, the being became the shradha of all and the Purusha is made up of shradha and his shradha is as he is. The Sattavic worshipped the God, the Rajsic worshipped the Yakshas and the Rakshasas and the Tamsic men worshipped the Pretas and the Bhutas. The men who practised frightful austerities (Tapas) unenjoined by the Shastras, wedded to hypocrisy and egoism, impelled by the force of desire (Kama) and affection (Raaga), senseless, tormenting the aggregates of the elements constituting the body and God too resting in the innermost body, such persons are of Asuric resolve. The food is also different for the persons of different Gunas. The food that increased vitality, essence, vigour, health, happiness, and are savoury of oleaginous, substantial and agreeable are dear to the Sattavic. Bitter, sour, saline, hot to excess, pungent, dry and burning food, productive of pain, grief and desire are desired by Rajsic and that which is cold, insipid, putrid and stale refuse even and unfit for Yagyas is the meal dear to Tamsic. The Yajna is Sattavic, which is performed by the non-fruit-desiring; which is in due form and with the mental conviction that it ought verily to be performed. With an eye, however, on the fruits and also for the sake of ostentation even, whatever is performed that Yajna is Rajsic and such Yajna is Tamsic which is devoid of due form, non-food-generating, mantraless and giftless and quite lacking in shradha. The Body Tapa is one in which one worshipped God, the twice-born, guru and the wise with purity, straightforwardness, Brahamcharya and harmlessness. The speech Tapa is the non-irritating which is also truthful, pleasant and beneficial and also constant study of Vedas. The Manas Tapa is the serenity of mind, gentleness, silence, perfect, self- controlled and purification of the nature. With supreme faith, that threefold Tapa performed by men, undesiring fruit and harmonised are Sattavic.

The Rajas are for the sake of respect, reverence and worship and even with hypocrisy. Further, the one of the deluded resolve, the Tapa which is performed with self-torture or for the sake of emotions' destruction are Tamsic. The gift made to one from whom no return is expected and in fit place and in time and to a fit person is Sattavic gift. What is, however, given with expectation of return or with an eye on fruits or reluctantly is Rajsic gift. The gift which is out of place and untimed and made to an unfit person with unwelcome and disdain is styled as Tamsic.

Krishna further stated that the renunciation of actions which are all karmas or seeking or desiring or having fruit is done by Sanyasis only and the abandonment of fruits of all actions is called Tyaga. Kama should be abandoned as evil as considered by the men who have controlled their Manas but the actions in the form of Yajna, Dana, Tapa ought not to be abandoned as opined by others. Further, Tyaga has been declared to be threefold. Actions in the form of Yajna, Dana and Tapa ought not to be abandoned as already indicated but should be continued to be done because they are the purifiers of the wise. These actions should, therefore, be continued to be done abandoning attachment and fruits and this opinion is considered to be the most certain and best.

Those who abandon actions from fear of bodily suffering are considered to be performing Rajsic Tyaga but such persons do not obtain the fruit of Tyaga. Therefore, it is necessary that the attachment and fruit should be abandoned taking that whatever action is ordained to be performed should be performed. Such a Tyaga is regarded as Sattavic. Thus the wise men who are Tyagis cut off their doubts they do not hate unpleasurable actions but continue to have attachment with the pleasurable ones. Men who cannot possibly abandon the fruits of actions are said to be Tyagis but the Tyagis attain the unwished for, wished for and mixed fruits of actions but can never become Sanyasis. In Sankhya philosophy, there are five causes to every action which come together before any action can show itself. These five factors or essentials of action are, the Adhisthana (Substraturm), the Karta (actor), the Karna (Instrument through which action can be done), the Chesta (Functioning) and the Daiva (Destiny). Every action is related to an individualised being on the plane of manifestation means the association of these five essential factors of action. These may also be called causes as they together cause the generation of actions. Action in the very first place presupposes the presence of a being, a manifested existence. There cannot be an action without there being a manifested existence and it is equally true that there cannot be a manifested existence that shall be without action in relation to it. Thus action and manifested existence go together. The five essential factors or causes are present in every manifested being and the centralised existence, the self, whose very existence becomes possible on account of the Adhisthana, which underlies him, is the Karta, acting through the Karana by virtue of the inherent functioning capacity endowed by the Rajas Guna and according to Daiva, which determines the mould of the Karana and the element of the functioning capacity (chesta). With the Chesta or the Rajsic tendency, inherent in the Karana enveloping the self, beginning its course towards objectivity, as determined by Daiva, action (Karma) is manifested. So whatever the nature of the actions which become manifested, they each and all have the five characters, Adhisthana, the Karta, the Karana, the Chesta and the Daiva and whatever action a man begins, right or wrong, by body, speech and manas, are these five and its causes. That being so, who verily from deluded Budhi sees the Atma as alone the actor, he is of perverted intelligence and does not see exactly.

Further, Gyan (Knowledge), Gyeye (what is to be known) and Gyata (Knower) are the threefold impulse to action; Karana (Instrument) Karma (action) and karta (Actor) are the threefold-aggregates (Constituents) of action. What is ordained by karma, devoid of attachment and without affection or hatred, performed by one undesiring fruit is called Sattavic and what karma, by desiring or with egoism is performed with a good deal of effort is styled as Rajsic and without minding the consequences, destruction, injury and capacity and not being away from delusion, whatever karma is undertaken that is said to be Tamsic. Also free from attachment, unegoistic, with firmness and zeal well endowed, by success or failure uninfluenced, such a Karta is called Sattvic and Rajsic is passionately attached, desiring the fruits of actions, greedy, essentially inclined to injury, moved by joy and grief.

Tamasic is one, who is unharmonised, unrefined, unyielding, deceitful, wicked, indolent, despairful and dilatory.

The Budhi which knows the difference between the Apravaritti and Nivaritti (Unrest and rest), what ought to be done (Karya) and what is not to be done (Akarya), fear and fearlessness, bondage and liberation, is Sattavic. Rajsic Budhi is one which does not know Dharma and Adharma, Karya and akarya as they are and the Tamsic Budhi is which being Tamas-enwrapped thinks Adharma to be the Dharma and all things subverted. The unswerving (Unadulterated) Dhriti (firmness) by which one holds the activities of Manas, the Pran and senses, is Sattavic Dhriti. But the Dhriti by which one form attachment, desirous of fruit, holds to Dharma, Karma and Artha, that Dhriti is Rajsic and the Dhriti by which one of perverted intelligence does not abandon sleep, fear, grief, despair and even intoxication is Tamsic. Now happiness too is of three kinds. The one which is like poison in the beginning and is nectar in the end is said to be Sattvic, which is born out of the serenity of Atma-Budhi (Self-centred Budhi); the Rajsic is one which is like nectar in the beginning and is like poison in the end by the union of senses and the sense-objects; the Tamsic is one in which happiness is deluded in the beginning and in the sequence. It springs from sleep, indolence and inaction. There is none, who is free from the Prakriti-born Gunas on the earth or in the Heaven among the gods. The actions of Brahmin, Kshatriya, Vaishas and Shudras are distinct arising from their own nature (swabhava).

The Brahmins karma, as born by their nature are control of Manas and senses, Tapa, purity, forbearance and also straightforwardness, knowledge, wisdom, faith in the existence of the Supreme. The Kshatriya karmas born of their nature are prowess, lustre, firmness, dexterity and also not running away from battle, gifts and lordly nature. Ploughing, protection of cows and trade are the Vaishyas' karma born of their nature and karma of essence of service is born out of the nature of Shudras. Krishna further tells how the one devoted to his own karmas attains perfection. From whom the activity (Pravaritti) of beings is pervaded by whom to the God with one's own karma worshipping, that individual attains perfection. One who performs Swabhava ordained karmas treating better his own Dharma, destitute of merit than another's Dharma is not tainted by sins. One, therefore, should not abandon the innate karma even if it is defective one. One attains the highest Sidhi (perfection) of actionlessness with Budhi unattached everywhere; the self controlled and desires dead and having attained Sidhi, one attains to Brahma, the Supreme attitude (Nishtha) of Gyan by being endowed with Budhi which is perfectly pure and with Dhriti well balancing the self, leaving the sense objects and giving up likes and dislikes, residing in solitude. Abstemious, with speech, body and mind controlled, constantly devoted to Dhyana (Meditation), Yoga, well-refuged in Vairagya (Non-attachment), having cast aside the egoism, force, pride, desire, anger, passions, devoid of "Mine-ness", peaceful and the

Brahmanised (One who has become Brahma), blissfully serene self, neither grieving nor having any desires, the same in all beings attains the God's Supreme and by devotion he knows what and who He is in essence, then knowing Him in essence he enters the Brahma immediately.

# Chapter XIX

## Taking Refuge in Him

With all actions performed after taking refuge in Him, one attains the imperishable eternal goal by His mercy. Thus intent on Krishna and not posing himself as Karta, he will make himself receptive of the influence flowing from the reality – the influence which will illumine his path towards Shri Krishna on whom he is intent. Between him and the object of his intentness is the region of Budhi, the Antakarana subtlest Ahankara Mahatattava with the Atma centralised therein and the infinite expanse of Mulprakriti. These are the obstacles in his way to Krishna on whom he is intent but through his grace he will overcome them all and cross beyond them to his goal, the Supreme Self. Thus for the "I" to attain to Krishna, he has to mentally renounce all actions i.e. turn away from the karana (Manas), step beyond his "I", rest in Budhi yoga and fix his Chitta on Shri Krishna i.e. not to turn to the coursing Rajas on the plane of Budhi or to anything that is not Shri Krishna. Failing in this attitude and remaining attached to his "I" and not looking beyond but continuing in touch with the Manas and the planes below, he will be destroyed. The destruction consists in his being doomed to manifestation where the influence of the Tamas to which he exposes himself destroys the essence of his self, veils his intelligence and cramps his powers. He will be subjected to repeated births and deaths in never-ending succession instead of the external life and peace which will be his if he followed Shri Krishna's advice and resting refuged in Budhi Yoga remained intent on Him. Thus Arjuna had to choose between his being inevitably forced to fight, with misery and bondage in return for his pains and his adopting Karma Yoga and allowing the fight – an attitude which could ensure him freedom and peace and attaining to Shri Krishna Himself. It was a senseless delusion, which prevented Arjuna from seeing his folly in the former and his interest in the latter. Thus Krishna had declared to Arjuna the Gyan, more secret than secrecy itself and asked him to ponder on this fully and then do as he liked. Again Krishna asked him to listen to further most secret of all which was his Supreme word and this he had been ready to tell him because Arjuna was his beloved and, therefore, he wished his welfare. Krishna told him to intent his Manas in him, he should be his devotee, his worshipper, bowing down to him and to him only he should come, so he would pledge his word to him. He should lay aside all Dharmas and come to him only for shelter and he would free him from all sins. Therefore, he should not have any grievance.

Thus rendering to him the secret of secret, Krishna left it to Arjuna to take a decision himself as to what he ought to do in the situation.

The Guru guides his disciple, removes his doubts, corrects his mistakes, explains to him what he is unable to understand, advises him, persuades him and shows him the path which he should follow but then it is for the disciple to act and do as he liked. The final decision as to what he should do rested always with him and it could not be enforced. That is what Krishna had done. If the disciple is not still able to take a decision, the Guru Shri Krishna feels the supreme word to Arjuna that he should rest his Manas in him, be devoted to him, worship him, bow down to him, come to him only for any help, pledge to him and he shall free him from all sins if he comes to him leaving all Dharmas and have shelter under him only. This is the torch-light to show the path of salvation to every being from the highest to the lowest. These attitudes include sanyas, Yoga, Bhakti, Sacrifice, Service and self-surrender and the ultimate absorption in him. Arjuna's fear of sin, Adharma etc. would now go as these were through ignorance which had been removed by Krishna. Any one, who having supreme devotion in Krishna, imparted the Supreme secret to any one shall attain him and in the human beings none shall be dearer to him on earth other than the one who imparted such secrets to others and who after studying the dialogue between Krishna and Arjuna, worshipped him with full faith and uncavilling, even the man who might hear it shall be liberated to the happy worlds of meritorious action and attain Him.

Krishna concludes his speech with the enquiry if Arjuna had heard all that had been said to him with unflagging attention and whether his delusion, the result of his ignorance, had completely gone. When Krishna began his speech, Arjuna was attached to his "I" and was strongly imbued with the sense of "I-ness". His mind was plunged in grief and he was deluded as to his Dharma. To cure Arjuna of his delusion, to remove the ignorance which clouded his intelligence, was the aim of the revelation made to him and, therefore, at the conclusion he enquires if his instruction has had the required effect. To have heard it is to have been in a receptive mood. The self must turn away from the Tamas which enveloped his "I" centralised in the Manas before he could hear to receive the revelation which came from the Supreme Self above. This was necessary for a Guru, as Krishna had been acting then to check up if while listening to him, he was so attentive as to be oblivious of his sense "I" because it was only when he stepped beyond his "I" that the glimpse from the Supreme came to him. Further, for perfect illumination and proper hearing one must further pass beyond the agitating Rajas as to have the first glimpse and the differentiating music he had to cross beyond his "I". Shri Krishna, when he asked Arjuna if he had listened to him with his Chitta made one-pointed, wanted to know if all the time, he was addressing him, Arjuna had been resting beyond his "I" and even beyond the Vritti of his Chitta differentiating and coursing on the region of Budhi. Imbued with sense of "I", when Arjuna threw his arms and abstained from fight, he was turned towards his Manas, the Karana, which enveloped his individuality or the "I" and beyond his "I" was the region of Gyan which linked him to the Gyeya above.

The karana to which he was turned obscured his Gyana. It was Arjuna and the cause of his delusion. To hear the revelation with Chitta made one-pointed, meant to have turned away from the enveloping Karana, the Manas, the cause of his ignorance and delusion and to have turned towards the Gyana and remained intent on the Gyana beyond the Gyana. This virtually came to this whether while listening to him, Arjuna had been resting centred in Sattava with his "I" sacrificed and free from the influence of the coursing Rajas on the plane of Budhi, and intent on the Gyeya, the reality from whom the voice came. To the enquiry of Krishna, Arjuna replied that his delusion had been destroyed since he listened with the Chitta made one-pointed and he had passed beyond in the region of Budhi and all this by the grace of the Lord. Arjuna further said that his memory had been restored, the differentiating plane of Budhi was the plane of his Vasanas, which were the differentiations of his nature, of the subtle mould of his Prakriti, which embodied his self centralised in the Sattava. When he, imbued with the sense "I" remained turned towards his Manas, the Tamas obtaining then veiled from him his real nature as he could not see anything beyond his "I". But when passing beyond his "I", he rested in the Sattava with his Chitta made one-pointed, the Tamsic veil was removed and he could see what he in essence was. Thus he remembered his real nature, his memory was restored – memory which had been lost by being veiled and obscured by Tamas.

When he now rested in Sattava, with his memory restored, he was free from all sense of duality and, therefore, from any doubt. So here as a result of his instruction, Arjuna's delusion and doubts had gone and the revelation had the desired effect and Arjuna's "I will not fight" was turned in to "I will do his bidding".

# SECTION II: MEDITATION

# Chapter XX

## Need of Meditation

The self is to be conquered by self and such a victorious self possessed to restraint and renunciation is a Yogi. It is achieved by complete conquest of Tamas. All objectivity is tinged with Tamas, more or less. From the objectivity, therefore, one must draw himself away and, in the subjectivity, only he must rest. This done he would have conquered the self and established himself a Yogi. All that a Yogi has to do is to continually centralise himself step by step, gathering himself in a Sattava away from the objectivity that seemed spread out before him till he reached the ultimate subjectivity. For this purpose at first he shall have to draw himself away from everything objective and when nothing on the objectivity affected him one way or the other, the avenues of his senses are closed to the variegated objectivity which surrendered him. For this he constantly thinks of nothing but himself as resting in his body in the objectivity from which he kept himself away.

Next is his body an objectivity no less objective and Tamas imbued than the rest of the objectivity from which he had turned away. He centralises his personality in the body. For this he just ceases to think of the surroundings as also the space where his very body rested i.e. he forgets that his body was in touch with the objectivity. This done he settles himself in a place perfectly pure, untouched and untinged by any Tamas from the surrendering objectivity. The three aspects of his body Tamsic, Rajsic and Sattavic corresponding to the three degrees of states of grossness of the matter constituting it are the three coverings – Kusha, Ajina (Skin of antelope) and a piece of cloth – spread out on his seat where on he rested at the top and centred in the last. With the personality so centred and turned away from the body he should make his Manas one-pointed. He should at that time be equally indifferent to the thought and memories vibrating in the Manas. This is to have the Chitta controlled. With the activities of the chitta and the senses so controlled, from the personality where he rested centred, he should have his Manas one-pointed i.e. centre himself in the Manas as the individuality or individual self. Thus centred he should devote himself to and engaged in Yoga for perfecting self-purification which he had commenced.

Centred in the Sattava of the Manas, he should turn away from the coursing Rajas reaching the objective personality below. His personality is the body or the trunk, the centre where he rested in the Manas is the head, the intervening plane of the Rajas is the neck connecting the two. Uninfluenced by the agitating Rajas, he should have all the three perfectly equipoised and steadied. He shall thus centre himself one-pointed and leave the Rajas alone.

For this purpose he shall have to fix his eyes on the individual self seeing nothing besides to the right or to the left, before or behind, above or below.

He is then steadied in Sattava, away from Rajas. Being so centred in the Sattava, he rests perfectly tranquil, seeing nothing besides his own individual self and not even experiencing the slightest agitation. So centred he rested firm in his vow to attain to Brahma, the ultimate Truth or perfect Bliss, or the ideal of his heart which he had set out in search of and which the sense of individuality, even if it was the most Sattavic, still kept him off. Thus the being in touch with the objectivity around him had to be thrice centralised before he became a Yogi or before the attainment of Supreme Nirvana. For this the being had to be centralised in the surrounding objectivity, the personality in the being and the individuality in the personality. So thrice centralised he is a Mumuksha who wished to be a Yogi had then to centralise the existence in the individuality and so centralised he rested intent on the Supreme and attained it. From the beginning to end everywhere and every time he had to repeat the same process. He drew himself away from the objectivity, overcame the Tamas, controlled his Chitta and the senses, overcame the agitating Rajas and rested centred in Sattava. When, with Chitta well controlled, in the self one rested, devoid of longing for all desires, then he is called harmonised and when the Chitta is restrained by the practice of yoga and when he also saw the self by the self in the self, then one felt satisfied. He then knew the Bliss Supreme apprehensible by the Budhi but beyond the senses and when established he does not waver from that supreme. When obtained he is not dislodged by even any pair and that is the disunion of the union with pair known as Yoga and that Yoga, with firm resolve engaged him with undespairing Chitta.

Then having abandoned the Kamas (desires) all without remnant by the Manas, verily having controlled the group of senses all around, by Budhi firmly held making the Manas rest in the self, without thinking of anything at all, when the Manas wandered away active and unsteady from those reining it in the self, it had to be subdued. Such a Yogi, with Manas perfectly calmed, the Rajas quitted himself Brahamanised and freed from impurity came the highest happiness. Thus constantly centralised the self, the Yogi, whose sins are gone, enjoyed the contact with Brahma the extreme happiness. The self harmonised in Yoga he saw sameness every where and saw the self abiding in all beings and all beings in the self. He saw gold everywhere.

It may further be stated that meditation is a transcendent virtue where we enter in to higher state of awareness and develop advanced accomplishments and powers. In this we get the ultimate freedom and full evolution of our minds and bodies and total transformation of our environment. After Pranayam, Renunciation, Concentration, we reach the stage of Meditation which is last but one stage from Samadhi, which is the ultimate aim of achieving the

Almighty. It gives us the mental stability and ends in reinforcing our ego-centrism. When we go on meditating for years, we reach the stage of deep concentration, which is meditation. Gita tells of meditation as essential element of daily chorus. This can be done any time during the day but it is preferably done in the morning when the mind is free from other worldly pre-occupations and one is fresh after taking bath etc.

Although we are constantly pre-occupied to the point where we feel that we do not have a single minute to spare, every minute having been booked, if not doubly booked, we have to carve out some time from our busy schedule taking this item to be as necessary for everyday indulgence. Therefore, morning time is suggested for this purpose aptly.

In Sanskrit it is also called "Dhyana" or the state of one-pointed concentration wherein the mind can focus on a chosen object or objective without veering away into distracting thought flows or sensory pre-occupation. For this purpose we need a new place to serve as a special refuge. It needs solitude in a beautiful place in nature and a modest but comfortable shelter filled with ample provisions. If such a situation is not attained, we can have it in the midst of our daily life in the evening when we are not too tired or in the morning before we are too stressed. For meditation one should find a corner in the house, sit there on an Asan, neither too low nor too high with folded legs. In front there should be an object of concentration like a statue or a picture of God (East), burn Agarbatti and Jyoti. These give a sense of being involved in meditation. In order to practise deep concentration, we must develop detachment from our obsession; have to learn to enjoy serene solitude, removing ourselves from all immediate distractions. Although our thought flow immediately returns to its familiar attachments, our bodies, other bodies, pleasures, possessions and experiences, but we have to drive it back as many times as it flows away. With repeated practice it is possible to keep it concentrated. To start with one may have a session of ten-twenty minutes and then increasing as one gets used to concentrate. Short bursts of focussed attention are the key to success with this practice. Once having started to concentrate one finds energy and bliss in freeing one's mind from addictive , involuntary thoughts and then joy will come effortlessly as our preserve through obstacles such as boredom, sleepiness and nervous frenzies.

# Chapter XXI

## Obstacles in Meditation

Now having been ready, first select an object that will be the focus of meditation. If one has a strong understanding of selflessness and can engage in the process of looking for self, turning back on it until one is spinning, dissolving, disappearing and re-appearing and sustain the non-finding of it, when one can select the self as the object of concentration. For this one should select an object of spiritual significance such as a painting, statue etc. and concentrate on it. Take it in hand, stare at it for some time until one is able to visualise it in every detail. Now close your eyes and the picture seems floating in front of your forehead, in front of the third eye (a place in forehead between the two eyes). Once you catch a glimpse of this image in your mind's eye, focus on it and let all other thoughts and images go. Do not be alarmed if after a few moments the image slips away and continue recollecting it again and again. Along the way as to attaining the full-fledged serenity of deep concentration, you will encounter five main obstacles – laziness, forgetfulness, boredom, non-reacting, and over-reacting.

For overcoming the first obstacle of laziness, you should cultivate your faith in the importance and power of serenity. Intelligence of concentration is fluid, constantly growing through challenging times or atrophying during times of disuse. So by practising intense concentration, you can systematically increase your brain power eliminating the element of laziness and make your serenity practice happen.

Forgetfulness is overcome by mindfulness. When you forget your object or even that you are practising one-pointed serenity concentration, you should focus all your attention on remembering the object of your meditation in detail, holding your mindfulness firmly on it and staying alert for oncoming distraction. Boredom is overcome by alertness. While on the main part of your concentration on the meditation object, keep another part of your mind secretly engaged in watching out for signs of sinking in boredom, alertness recharges you by reminding you of the benefits of serenity. In non-reacting, the object of your meditation gets lost and you find yourself unmoved by your concentration of bliss, joy and serenity. You must go back to some of the most basic motivational meditation and rekindle your interest in enlightenment. When your mind is freshened up return your awareness to the object of your meditation and if you still feel non-reacting then have a break, wash your face with cold water, do some Yoga postures and return to meditation when you feel reinspired. Similarly, over-reacting is overcome by equal-mindedness. For this you must introduce moderation and balance in to all your mental efforts so that you do not allow yourself to become over-stimulated. The most efficient way to do this is to think about suffering, death etc., which will stabilise your mind by making you more serious. If it does not work then try counting your in-out breath cycles up to ten, twenty or one hundred if necessary and keep on repeating the counting till you reach the target number without distraction. Be calm and collected again return your attention to the meditation object.

Once all these obstacles get resolved, you will be able to have deep concentration pointedly and joyously. Your selfless being is totally saturated with bliss and at the same time your mind remains completely undisturbed in its focus on your chosen object and you feel non-duality. At this point the deep concentration becomes effortless. It is important however, that you should not become complacent once you attain this advanced level of serenity as still you are away from the last stage of attaining Samadhi crossing over from meditation. It is through Samadhi only that one can hope of reaching the 'Moksha', the ultimate aim of all human beings. However, with the deep concentration you develop greater and greater mental powers and will become far more capable of helping others than you ever were before. Once having been aware of the deep concentration, you can be on way to achieving full fledged serenity but for this, complete renunciation from worldly involvements is necessary for which you can go step by step with determined effort by increasing the time of deep concentration from twenty minutes to forty minutes and so on. Each time you are able to count a few more breaths without destruction, see the image of your object a bit more clearly or experience slightly deeper focus and congratulate yourself for having done an excellent job.

Everyone wants happiness. Yet a few of us seem to find it. In our search for satisfaction, we go from one relationship to another, one job to another or one country to another. We study at medicine, train to be players, have babies, cars, write books and grow flowers. We spend our money on home entertainment system, mobile phones, comfortable furniture or we try to get back to nature, eat whole foods, practice Yoga and meditate. Whatever we do is an attempt to find real happiness and avoid suffering but we do not attain. The problem is that we see things like relationships, possessions and adventures as having some intrinsic ability to satisfy us, as being the cause of happiness. But they cannot be simply because they do not last. Even our body does not last. But till the body and mind are there, people will go on thinking about getting happiness. Mind changes from moment to moment. It is a beginningless continuum, like an ever-flowing stream; the previous mind-moment gave rise to this mind-moment, which gives rise to the next mind-moment and so on. It is the general name given to the totality of our conscious and unconscious experiences; each of us is a centre of a world of thoughts, perceptions, feelings, memories and dreams – all of these are mind, which can be compared to an ocean and momentary mental events such as happiness, irritation, fantasies and boredom to the waves that rise and fall on its surface. Just as waves cannot subside to reveal the stillness of the ocean's depth, so it is not possible to calm the turbulence of our mind to reveal its natural pristine clarity.

# Chapter XXII

## Control of Mind

The mind can be divided into sense consciousness - sight, hearing, smelling, taste and touch – and mental consciousness. Mental consciousness ranges from our grossest experience of anger or desire. Meditation is an activity of the mental consciousness. It involves one part of the mind observing, analysing and dealing with the rest of mind. Meditation can take many forms - concentrating single-pointedly on an internal object, trying to understand some personal problems, generating a joyful love for all humanity, praying to an object of devotion or communicating with our inner wisdom. Its ultimate aim is to awaken a very subtle level of consciousness and to use it to discover reality, directly and intuitively. This direct, intuitive awareness of how things are, combined with love and compassion for all beings, is known as enlightenment. Meditation is not an activity of body, it is not simply a matter of sitting in a particular posture or breathing a particular way, nor is it done for the purpose of experiencing pleasant bodily sensations. Rather, it is an activity of the mind, making it more positive. First we learn to develop the meditative state of mind in formal sitting practice but once we are good at it, we can be more free-style and creative and can generate this mental state at any time and in any situation. By then meditation would become a way of life. The mind has positive and negative aspects. The negative aspects are our mental disorders or quite literally delusions, including jealousy, anger, desire, pride and the like. These arise from our misunderstanding of reality and habitual clinging to the way we see things. Through meditation we can recognise our mistakes and adjust our mind to think and react more realistically and more honestly. The final of enlightenment is a long term one but meditation done with this goal in mind can and do have enormous short-term benefits.

Meditation can be stabilizing and analytical. Stabilizing meditation is used to develop concentration and eventually to attain calm-abiding, a special type of concentration that enables one to remain focussed on whatever object one wishes for as long as one wishes, while experiencing bliss, clarity and peace. Concentration and calm-abiding are necessary for any real, lasting insight and mental transformation. In stabilizing meditation, we learn to concentrate upon one object – the breath, the nature of one's own mind, a concept, a visualised image – without interruption.

Analytical meditation is for the purpose of developing insight, or correct understanding of the way things are and eventually to attain special insight that sees the ultimate nature of all things. Analytical meditation brings in to play creative, intellectual thought and is crucial to our development - the first step in gaining any real insight is to understand conceptually how things are. This conceptual clarity develops in to firm conviction which, when combined with stabilizing meditation, brings direct and intuitive knowing. Gradually we can eliminate those thoughts, feelings and ideas that cause ourselves and others unhappiness and in their place cultivate thoughts, feelings and ideas that bring happiness and peace. In this way we become familiar with the reality of cause and effect – that our present experiences are the result of our past actions and the cause of our future experiences. This method of combining the two kinds of meditation causes the mind literally to become one with the object of meditation and the stronger our concentration, the deeper our insight will be.

In order to experience the benefits of meditation it is necessary to practice regularly, as with any activity, it is not possible to succeed unless we dedicate our energy whole-heartedly to it. For this, meditation has to be done every day for some time, to be increased gradually. If possible, it is best to reserve a room or a corner, specially, for the meditation sessions. Set up the seat, either a cushion or on floor, on a bed or sofa or a straight-backed chair, with a table or low bench in front for this and other books that may be needed for meditation. One can also set up an altar nearby for statues or pictures that inspire him. Ideally the place should be clean and quiet, so that we are not disturbed. However, with discipline it is possible to meditate in a crowded, noisy environment; people in prison, for example, often cannot find a quiet place and still become successful meditators. It is good to start with the meditation on the breath. This is ideal for calming the mind and starting to develop some insight in to our thoughts and feelings – and both calm and insight are essential ingredients for successful meditation of any kind. Once we are familiar with meditation, we can choose practices that best suit our needs remembering that all the techniques here are either antidotes to particular problems or methods for enhancing particular qualities.

If, for example, we are inclined towards anger, we can meditate on patience or loving kindness. If disturbed by strong desire or attachment, we would be benefitted from meditating on impermanence, death or suffering. Depression can be counter-acted by thinking about the preciousness and potential of our human life. Often we feel that things happen randomly or that life is unfair, if so, meditation on karma be done. If we regret the harm we had done to others or feel hopeless and do not believe we can change, do one of the purification practices. If we are overwhelmed by the suffering of the world and want to develop the courage to help others, we should meditate on compassion and gracefulness. During meditation our mind and body should be relaxed and comfortable throughout the session. We can relax mentally deciding to leave behind all problems, worries and involvements of the external world and immerse ourselves in our inner world. Breathing meditation can also bring the same result. Since we all want to enjoy happiness and peace of mind and avoid problems, it is natural to want good experiences during meditation and whenever we discover something new and interesting we would feel like telling everyone about it but it is not a good idea to talk too much about the meditation, unless someone is sincerely interested and asks us about it, it is better to keep quiet. Broadcasting our experiences will dissipate whatever good energy and insight we have gained. Meditation is an internal, not external activity. Our practice shall transform our mind on a stable level, making us more sensitive and clear and giving us fresh insight in to ordinary day-to-day experiences.

# Chapter XXIII

## Position for Meditation

Our mind and body are inter-dependent because the state of one affects the state of the other and a correct sitting posture has been emphasised for meditation. The seven point posture, as given below, is recommended as the best:

**Legs:** The best position for meditation is the Vajra position where we sit cross-legged with each foot placed, sole upward, on the thigh of the opposite leg. But if one is not able to do it an alternative position is the half lobis where the left foot is on the floor under the right leg and right foot on top of the left thigh or sit in simple cross-legged posture with both feet on the floor. We should have a mat or a carpet beneath us and a cushion or two under the buttocks will enable us to sit comfortably for longer periods. If it is not possible to sit then chair etc. can also be used.

**Arms:** Hold the hands loosely on the lap, about two inches below the navel, right hand on top of the palms upward with the fingers aligned. The two hands should be cupped so that the tips of the thumbs meet to form a triangle. Shoulders and arms should be relaxed and the arms should not be pressed against the body but held a few inches away to allow circulation of air. This also helps to prevent sleepiness.

**Back:** It should be straight, held relaxed and lightly upright.

**Eyes:** It is easier to concentrate with eyes fully closed. However, it is recommended that the eyes can be left slightly open to admit a little light and direct the gaze downward as closing the eyes may be an invitation to sluggishness, sleep or dreamlike images, which hinder meditation.

**Jaw:** Jaw should be relaxed and teeth slightly apart, not clenched. Mouth should be relaxed also with lips together lightly.

**Tongue:** The tip of the tongue should touch the palate just behind the upper teeth. This reduces the flow of saliva and thus the need to swallow, both of which could be distracting.

**Head:** Neck should be bent forward a little so that the gaze is directed naturally towards floor in front. If the head is held too high, it may create problems with mental wandering and agitation and if dropped too low we could experience mental heaviness or sleepiness.

This seven-point posture is most conducive to clear, unobstructed contemplation. We might find it difficult in the beginning but it is good idea to check every point at the start of the session and try to maintain the correct posture for a few minutes in the beginning to be increased slowly.

At times during the meditation, the mind is very restless and our attention is continually distracted by other things. These can include external objects like sounds but also internal distractions such as memories of the past, fantasies about the future, incessant chatter about what is happening in the present. Such thoughts are often accompanied by disturbing emotions such as attachment, anger or hatred. It is not easy to give up habits but we should recognise that this mental excitement is the very opposite of meditation. There are a number of methods for counter-acting mental excitement. One is to focus firmly on the breath and let the mind become as calm as the natural rhythm of our breathing. Every time the attention wanders, it has to be brought back to the breath. But if the mind is strongly caught up in a disturbing emotion such as attachment or anger, it might be necessary to spend some time working with one or more of the antidotes to these and once the control is regained on mind, we can return to the meditation. If mental restlessness is a recurring problem, we should check our posture. The spine should be very straight and the head tilted slightly forward with the chin tucked slightly in - the mind tends to be more restless when the head is raised too high. Reducing the amount of light in the room could also help, as bright light can stir up thoughts and feelings. When there is sleepiness, then we should make sure that our back is straight and our head is not bent forward too far. The eyes should be opened half-way and should meditate with our gaze directed at the floor in front of us. Increasing the amount of light in the room should also help to stay alert or we can splash cold water on our face, get some fresh air or do some stretching or stop the meditation altogether and try again later.

The meditation will flow smoothly if our body is relaxed and comfortable but often it is difficult to get it in to that state. Much of our physical attention is mind related arising from unresolved problems, fears, worries or anger. The most effective solution for this is to recognise these problems and settle them in meditation. A short term method of easing physical tension is to sweep the body with our attention, then concentrate briefly on each part and consciously let it relax and imagine that the tension is simply dissolved. Another method is to breathe deeply and slowly and with much concentration we should imagine that the tension or pain leaves our body with each exhalation. Further, if sitting causes discomfort or pain – in the knees or back - it is all right to change to a more comfortable position.

Although it is best to meditate in the quiet place, it is not always possible to find one. In the city we find traffic, T.V., music, kids playing, people talking, aeroplanes passing overhead etc. but even out in the country or high on the mountain, there are sounds of birds or animals, the wind blowing, a stream or a river noise but the problem is not so much of the noise itself but rather how our mind reacts to it. If the noise is pleasant, such as music we like, we feel attracted and want to pay attention to it rather than our object of meditation, i.e. attachment. If the noise is unpleasant, we feel irritation or aversion. Either way we get struck to the noise and it is difficult to let go of it and carry on with the meditation. The best way to deal with this situation is to recognise what is happening in our mind and heart to just be aware of the noise without reaching to it. Once we do this, we generate a strong, positive motivation at the beginning of our session so that we feel joyful and enthusiastic about meditating. Meditation as such is the way to purify the mind of what is already there; at first we discover the gross negatives and then the more stable ones. As already mentioned one kind of meditation i.e. stabilizing meditation is for the purpose of developing concentration. Concentration is the natural quality of our mind. As the goal of spiritual practice is freeing our minds from negative thoughts and emotions and attaining perfect clarity, peace and joy, we need to learn to concentrate our minds on positive, beneficial objects. Stabilizing meditation involves focussing the mind on an object and bringing it back whenever it wanders away. There are several qualities of the mind that are essential in developing good concentration. One of these is mindfulness or recollection, which enables us to remember a familiar object (like our breath) without forgetting it or wandering to other objects. Mindfulness also enables us to keep in mind what we are supposed to be doing while we are sitting there and not to get completely spaced out. Another essential quality is discriminating alertness, which, like a sentry, watches out for distraction atleast knows what is happening moment by moment. Mindfulness and alertness are thus essential for successful meditation and in our day-to-day lives they keep us centred, alert and conscientious, helping us to know what is happening in our mind as it happens and then to deal skilfully with problems as they arise. For this we have to decide how long we would meditate and determine that for the duration of the session we will keep our attention on the breath in order to fulfil the purpose and then focus our mind on our breathing.

We should not try to control our breath, we should just breathe normally and gently. We should be content to stay in the present and accept whatever frame of mind we are in and whatever arises in our mind, without judging it as good or bad. We should be free of expectations, clinging and frustration. When our skills have developed in this direction and our ability to avoid distraction has increased, we can take our alertness a step further. Make mental notes of the nature of the thoughts that arise, such as thinking, memory, fantasy, feeling angry, attachment, hearing a sound, feeling bored or having pain. As soon as we have noted the thoughts or feelings, we should let it go, recalling its impermanent nature. When it is time to end the session, we should feel good about what we have done. Just making an effort to meditate is in itself very meaningful and beneficial. We should rejoice in the positive energy we have generated and dedicate it to the benefit of all beings.

# Chapter XXIV

## Reconciliation of Body and Mind

The reality of our existence is that we are a combination of body and mind. Each of these in turn is a combination of many parts, all constantly in a state of flue. Unfortunately our ego is not satisfied with such a simple explanation. It complicates matters by fabricating a view of an "I" or self based on our conceptions, likes and dislikes. Meditation or the clarity of mind is an effective antidote to our concrete projections. We can gain a direct experience of the clear, non-material transient nature of all thoughts, feelings and perceptions, thus weakening the tendency to identify with them. The meditation is especially effective for softening our view of ourselves and consistent practice of the meditation will eventually generate a certainty about this pure nature to the point where it becomes our reality, our actual experience. This is a natural step towards understanding the more stable nature of self and all phenomena, their emptiness and inherent existence. We, however, must have a positive motivation for doing meditation. Our consciousness, or mind, is whatever we are experiencing at the moment i.e. sensation in our body, thoughts, feelings, perceptions of sounds and so forth. The nature of each of these experiences is clarity, without form or colour, space-like, pure awareness. We should focus our attention on this clear, pure nature of mind. Thoughts and distractions will continue to arise but we should not react to them neither follow them nor reject them and should not think about anything during the meditation as concentration means holding the mind on an object continuously, without forgetting it. The automatic result of concentration is awareness, which is free of concepts.

For this purpose mind has been compared to a vast ocean, and our perceptions, thoughts and emotions to waves rising and falling on its surface. This analogy helps us to understand the experiences that occur while we are meditating to going about our daily activities. But to get a feeling for where the mind comes from and where it goes to, it is useful to think of it as a river flowing through time. Here are several analytical approaches to considering the validity of mental continuity. The mind is impermanent, transitory, changing from moment to moment. Thus it is in effect, a result of the product of causes and conditions and the main cause of a mind is necessarily a previous moment of mind. Causes and their results must be the same type of phenomena.

So it is not possible for mind, a nonphysical phenomenon, to arise or be produced from a physical phenomena such as the body, just as it is not possible for fire to be produced by water. It is also not possible for a part of our mind to break off and become a new mind. Also, if our mind did come from our parents' minds, then would not we be born with all of their memories and knowledge. This is clearly not the case. Our present personality, knowledge and experience are necessarily the result of our past experiences and actions. Our mind, therefore, comes from its own previous continuity. For practising meditation, we should sit comfortably and relax, then contemplate a positive, beneficial motivation for doing the meditation, then spend some time concentrating on our breath, until the mind is quiet and clear. At first we should take a look at our present state of mind, at the thoughts and sensations flashing by. Just observe them in a detached way without clinging to or rejecting any of them. We should consider these possibilities carefully, using the reasons given earlier. Although we might not come to any definite conclusion, the important thing is to look with a clear and open mind. All religious teachings are for the purpose of leading one gradually to the realisation of emptiness. Here emptiness means the emptiness of inherent, concrete existence and total eradication from our mind of this false way of seeing things marks our achievement of enlightenment. In practical terms emptiness of inheritance existence means the one in which all things are said to lack to be empty of and is a quality that we instinctively project on to every person and everything we experience.

Take a table for example. We see a solid. Independent table standing before us and it is so obviously a table that it seems ridiculous to even question it. But where is the table? Imagine taking it apart and laying the pieces out on the ground. Now see if we can find the table. We only see its legs and top. On investigating thoroughly we find that we simply cannot find the table we thought was there. It does not mean that there is no table at all. There is a dependently-existing, changing from moment to moment, table that we merely label on to its parts. Similarly we experience not the bare reality of each thing and each person but an exaggerated, filled out image of it projected by our own mind. This pervasive mental disorder starts with the misapprehension of our own self. We are a composite body – a man of flesh, bones, skin, cells, atoms and mind with a stream of thoughts, feelings and perceptions. This composite is conveniently known as woman, man, Ram etc. It is a temporary alliance that ends with the death of the body and the flowing of the mind to other experiences. Our adherence to the false "I", known as self-grasping ignorance, taints all our dealings with the world. We are attracted to people, places and situations that gratify and uphold our self-image and react with fear or animosity to whatever threatens it. We view all people and things as definitely this way or that way. Thus this root, self-grasping, branches out into attachment, jealousy, anger, arrogance, depression, and the myriad other turbulent and unhappy states of mind.

The final solution is to eliminate this root ignorance – with the wisdom that realises the emptiness, in everything we experience -

of the false qualities we project on to things. This is the ultimate transformation of mind. Emptiness sounds pretty abstract understanding and get an idea of what it is, we think, exists; to locate, for example, the "I" that we believe in so strongly and then by using clear reasoning in analytical meditation, to see that it is a mere fabrication, something that has never existed and could never exist in the first place. Therefore, we should begin with a meditation on the breath to relax and calm our mind. Motivate ourselves strongly to do this meditation in order to finally become enlightened for the sake of all beings. The mind is a constantly changing stream of thoughts, feelings and other experiences, coming and going in rapid succession. It is never the same from one moment to the next. Which of those experiences is "I"- a loving thought, an angry thought, a happy feeling or a depressed feeling, if we think our "I" is the one of these experiences, then what happens to it when that kind of experience is not present in our mind and if our "I" is love, for example, then when our mind is filled only with anger, does the "I" go somewhere else or disappear altogether? Is there no "I" at that time? Or maybe we have many "Is", an angry one, a loving one, a frightened one etc. We have to see if there is some extra part of us other than our own body and mind as after all we say "My body" and "My mind" implying the existence of some thing else that owns these two. If so, what it is, where it is found and what kind of phenomena it is? We have to examine this. Again look at the way our "I" actually appears, how do wethen feel, do we feel any change or still believe that it is as solid and real as we felt before or does it still appear to exist independently, in and of itself. Next, if we mentally disintegrate on body and imagine all the atoms separating and floating apart, billions and billions of minute particles would scatter throughout space and thus imagine if we can actually see this. We should at the same time not make the mistake of thinking, "My body "is not the "I" and "my mind "is not the "I", therefore, I do not exist. But actually we exist but not in the way we instinctively feel as some thing independent and inherent.

Actually this is "us" that is sitting and meditating and wondering whether or not we exist. So conventionally things exist dependently and understanding dependence is the principle cause for understanding their ultimate nature i.e. emptiness. Now think that this meditation is just one step along the path to finally achieving direct insight in to emptiness and thus cutting the root of suffering and dis-satisfaction. The meditation is one antidote to negative states of being such as depression and hopelessness. It helps us to recognise and rejoice in our good fortune, in our extraordinary and unique potential to achieve true happiness and satisfaction and an understanding of this potential naturally fills us with joy and enthusiasm of life. We can unlock the potential for happiness and satisfaction that lies within every one of us by becoming aware of our mental processes and then applying discriminating wisdom to all our actions of body, speech and mind.

Once we understand this, we can begin to train our minds to achieve enlightenment. Thus begin the meditation by contemplating that the nature of your mind is clear and pure, and has the potential to become enlightened. Alternately, if we find it difficult to accept that the mind has the potential to become enlightened, we can think of the positive qualities that we have viz. intelligence, loving, kindness, compassion, generosity, courage etc. and remind ourselves that these can be developed even further and that we can use our lives to bring benefit and happiness to others.

Some people do not have access to spiritual teachings that explain the mind's potential and how to develop it. He should imagine spending his entire life in a small remote village where no one has even heard about enlightenment, so there is no opportunity to learn how to attain it. Other people may be aware of their potential and sincerely wish to practise the teachings on how to develop it but are prevented by others from doing so. For example, people in some countries do not have freedom of religion, others face strong objection from their parents, spouse or children. We should imagine ourselves in such a situation, recognise how difficult it would be and appreciate the freedom that we have. Some people engage in harmful actions such as killing, stealing, being abusive or dishonest, not realising that these actions cause suffering to themselves and others and create further obstacles to discovering their true potential. In such a situation we should bring to mind the positive qualities and advantages we have. We are human beings with an intelligent mind, a loving heart and a body we can put to good use and there are people who can care about and support us viz. our family, friends, a spiritual teacher and so we have opportunities to pursue our creative, intellectual and social interests enjoying a good standard of living. Now once we have seen the disadvantages, our life is free of and the advantages we enjoy we have to decide how best to use our precious opportunities.

Everything in the physical world is impermanent, changing all the times. Some changes are obvious like people grow up, get old and die, buildings and bridges wear out and fall apart. The environment goes through a complete transformation from one season to the next, flowers wilt, paints crack and pelt, cars break down etc. The source of this external transformation can be traced to the cellular and molecular composition of matter, where change is not so obvious. At this invisible level, minute particles are constantly coming into or going out of existence, gathering and dispersing and contacting. Our conscious world is also changing constantly. Some times we are happy, sometimes we feel full of love and other times full of anger. Such constant change is the reality of things but we find it very difficult to accept. Take for instance the body. On a subtler level, all the parts of our body are made of molecule, atoms and sub-atomic particles and these are in constant motion. We should try to really get a feeling for the change that is taking place every moment in our body. Now turn the attention to mind. It too is composed of many parts viz. thoughts, feelings, perceptions, memories and images following one after the other ceaselessly. Here again we would observe and try to get a sense of the impermanence, ever changing nature of our mind.

After reflecting the impermanence of our inner world, our body and mind, we now extend our awareness to the outer world. If we think about our immediate surroundings, the cushion, mat or bed, we are sitting on, the floor, walls, windows and ceiling of the room, the furniture and other objects in the room, all these appear solid and static but are actually a mass of tiny particles whizzing around. Now let the awareness travel further out, beyond the walls of the room. If we think of other people, their bodies etc. they are constantly changing and not staying the same even for a moment. The same is true of all living beings such as animals, insects, birds etc. If we think of all the inanimate objects in the world and in the universe, houses, buildings, roads, cars, trees, mountains, oceans all these things being composed of atoms and other minute particles are constantly changing. Therefore, it is unrealistic and self-defeating to cling to things as though they were permanent. Whatever is beautiful and pleasing will change and will eventually disappear, so we cannot expect it to give us lasting happiness. Also, whatever is unpleasant or disturbing will not last forever. It might even change for the better. So there is no need to be upset or to reject it. Besides the above processes of meditation there is meditation on death. When we are first confronted with the idea of meditating on death, we might react with shock. Perhaps, we think that meditation should deal with good experiences whereas death and things associated with it – tears of grief, black clothing, skeletons and cemeteries – evoke feelings of fear and panic. We see death as the contradiction of life, beauty and happiness it belongs to the realm of the unmentionable or the unthinkable. But we should not have such unrealistic attitudes. We should be able to accept death as calmly as we accept yesterdays, fresh flowers wilting today. Change, disintegration and death are natural, inevitable aspects of existence. We explain death as the separation of mind (Atma) and body after which the body disintegrates and the mind continues to another life. The "I" that depends on the present mind-body combination, ends at death. Death is, therefore, not a cessation but a transition or a transformation. At the root of our easiness and denial is ignorance. We cling to our self-image as something permanent and unchanging and want to live forever. This is not to imply that there is something wrong with trying to stay alive as life is indeed very precious. But it would be useful to examine the nature of the "I" that does not want to die.

# Chapter XXV

## Inevitability of Death

The understanding of emptiness, discussed above, or the non-existence of an inherent, permanent self frees us from fear of death and from all fears and misconceptions. Unless that point is reached, however, it is important to maintain awareness of impermanence and death. The principal benefit of practising this meditation is that it forces us to decide what attitudes and activities are truly worth-while. Death can happen any time and to die without undertaking the only work that has any long-lasting benefit either to ourselves or to others would be highly regrettable. How we live our lives inevitably affects how we die. If we live peacefully we will die with peace. There is, therefore, no need whatsoever to regard death with fear or sorrow. It can in fact be an enlightening experience. There are various ways of meditating on death like taking in to account:

1. The inevitability of death.
2. The uncertainty of the time of death.
3. The fact that only spiritual insight can help us at the time of death.

These need no explanation and we can meditate on these points one by one or all together. When our mind is calm and settled in the present, we should generate a positive motivation for doing the meditation. We plan many activities and projects for the coming days, months and years. Although death is the only event that is certain to occur, we do not usually think about it or plan for it. Even if the thought of death does arise in our mind, we usually push it away quickly. We should in this connection contemplate on following points:

1. <u>Everyone has to die:</u> to generate an experience of death's inevitability, first bring to mind people from the past like famous rulers, writers, saints, philosophers and ordinary people. These people were once alive. They worked, thought, wrote, fought, enjoyed life and suffered and finally died. Now bring to mind the people we know who have already died and think of people who are still alive. Contemplate that every one of these people will die and so shall we.

2. <u>The life-span is decreasing continuously:</u> Time never stands still, it is continuously passing and as time passes we travel closer and closer to death and this is the reality that we constantly move towards death and we can do nothing to avoid or postpone it.

3. <u>The amount of time spent during our life to develop our mind is very small:</u> Given that the mind alone continues

after death, the only thing that will be of any value when we die is the positive and constructive energy we have created during our life. By meditating on the above points, we should be able to develop the determination to use our life wisely and mindfully.

4. <u>The uncertainty of the time of death:</u> By contemplating on the above points, we accept that we are definitely going to die but we might think that death is not going to happen for a long time. There is no way we can know for sure when death will happen.

5. <u>Human life expectancy is uncertain:</u> If human beings died at a specific age say eighty years, we would have plenty of time and space to prepare for death but there is no such certainty and death catches most of us by surprise. Life can end at any point, at birth, in childhood, in adolescence at the age of 30, 40, 50 and so on. We, therefore, have to generate a strong feeling of the complete uncertainty of our time of death.

6. <u>There are many causes of death:</u> There are many different ways that death happens to people like due to external cause like natural disasters, earthquakes, floods or accidents, murders, terrorists riots etc. In internal causes death can come by different human diseases or old age etc. and we should think that these things could happen to us as well.

7. **The human body is very fragile:** Our human body is very vulnerable, it can be injured or struck down by illness so easily and within minutes it can change from being strong and active to being helplessly weak and full of pain and die.

8. **The fact that only spiritual insight can help us at the time of death:** No matter how much we have acquired or developed through out our life in terms of family, friends, wealth, power and so on but none of these go with us at death. The only things that will truly benefit us at the time of death are positive states of mind such as faith, non-attachment and calm acceptance of the changes that are taking place, loving, kindness, compassion, patience and wisdom.

9. **Your loved ones cannot help:** When we face difficult or frightening situations, our thoughts usually turn to our loved ones; our friends and our families. However, it is not certain that they will be there because you might die far from home. And even if they are present with us at the time of death, they may not be able to help us although they might have been loving us and may not like us to die but they cannot prevent from this happening and when we die, we go alone, no one, not even our closest, dearest loved ones can accompany us. Then we have to recognise the attachment we have to our family and friends and realise that having strong attachment to people can only be a hindrance to having a peaceful state of mind at the time of

death. So, it is better to work on decreasing the attachment and learning to let go.

10. <u>Our possessions and enjoyments cannot help:</u> Our mind will also probably think of our possessions and property which occupy a great deal of our time while we were alive and are a source of much pleasure and satisfaction but they too can not bring any comfort at the time of death. Rather our mind might be caught up in worries about them as to who will get what and whether or not they shall take proper care of "our" things and that will make it difficult to have a peaceful, detached state of mind as we are dying.

11. <u>Our own body cannot help:</u> Our body has been our constant companion since birth. We know it more intimately than anything or anyone else. We have cared for it and protected it, worried about it, kept it comfortable and healthy, fed it and cleaned it but at the time of death we are separated from it and the same body turns in to ashes. Contemplate the strong sense of dependence and attachment we had to our body and how it can not benefit us at the time of death rather we regret it leaving us.

By meditating on the above points, we should come to realise how important it is to work on reducing our attachment to the things of life such as our family, friends, possessions and our body itself. We also realise how important it is to take care of our mind as that is the only thing that will continue to the next life. Although fear arises because of clinging to the idea of a permanent self, yet there is no such thing, so this is a delusion that just makes us suffer and this we have to get rid off for all time to come if we want to be at peace in the remaining part of our life or even at the time of death.

---

# The Author

Hailing from Haryana, the author Mr. D.D Agarwal was born in 1933. He did his schooling from Sonepat and had further education from Delhi. Having been recruited through IAS & Allied Services examination, he retired as Joint Secretary from Ministry of Railways in 1994. After retirement he started writing books as pastime and has already written many books including:

- Protocol in Ramcharitmanas (in English and Hindi)
- Protocol in Srimad Bhagwat (in English and Hindi)
- Protocol in Mahabharata
- Upanishadas – The Real Truth
- India Ever Independent: Why Only Fifty Years
- Judisprudence in India Through Ages

The present book, Karma, Dharma and Meditation is the latest addition in the series. Of late he has started writing poems in Hindi and has a collection of over 1000 poems, mostly on spiritualism.

www.ingramcontent.com/pod-product-compliance
Lightning Source LLC
LaVergne TN
LVHW010203070526
838199LV00062B/4484